CONTENTS

Airborne – Battles That Changed History

MAIN COVER IMAGE: guvendemir/Getty Images

PHOTO CREDITS: The authors have attempted where possible to trace the copyright holders of all the images. Any errors will be corrected in future editions.

ABOVE: By Air to Battle. A British paratrooper prepares to land during a training exercise in 2022. (MOD/CROWN COPYRIGHT)

ABOVE: The US Army's use of helicopters in the Vietnam conflict in the 1960s showed the potential of large scale deployment of air mobile forces in battle. (US NATIONAL ARCHIVES)

ISBN: 978 1 80282 628 9

Editor: Tim Ripley

Senior editor, specials: Roger Mortimer

Email: roger.mortimer@keypublishing.com

Cover Design: Dan Hilliard

Design: SJmagic Design Services, India

Advertising Sales Manager: Brodie Baxter

Email: brodie.baxter@keypublishing.com

Tel: 01780 755131

Advertising Production: Debi McGowan

Email: debi.mcgowan@keypublishing.com

SUBSCRIPTION/MAIL ORDER
Key Publishing Ltd, PO Box 300, Stamford, Lincs, PE9 1NA
Tel: 01780 480404
Subscriptions email: subs@keypublishing.com
Mail Order email: orders@keypublishing.com
Website: www.keypublishing.com/shop

PUBLISHING
Group CEO: Adrian Cox
Publisher, Books and Bookazines: Jonathan Jackson
Head of Marketing: Shaun Binnington

Published by
Key Publishing Ltd, PO Box 100, Stamford, Lincs, PE9 1XQ
Tel: 01780 755131
Website: www.keypublishing.com

PRINTING
Precision Colour Printing Ltd, Haldane, Halesfield 1, Telford, Shropshire. TF7 4QQ

DISTRIBUTION
Seymour Distribution Ltd, 2 Poultry Avenue, London, EC1A 9PU
Enquiries Line: 02074 294000.

ABOVE: German airborne forces were the first paratroopers to see action in World War Two. (SEALAND PHOTOS)

A new generation of paratroopers are learning to jump from the new A400M Atlas airlifter. (MOD/CROWN COPYRIGHT)

Airborne Battles

Elite Forces in Action

FAR RIGHT: Lance Corporal Joshua Leakey, 27, of the British Parachute Regiment, was awarded the Victoria Cross, the UK's premier award for gallantry in the presence of the enemy during combat operations in Afghanistan in 2013. The regiment's famous red beret has been adopted by airborne units around the world.

RIGHT: Italian army soldier Alessandro Tandura was the first combat paratrooper who jumped behind Austrian lines in 1918 in a bid to scout out enemy positions. (PRIVATE COLLECTION)

It takes a special kind of soldier to parachute or land by helicopter behind enemy lines in the dead of night, with little food and only as much ammunition as they can stuff into a small rucksack. If this is not enough, then airborne troops need to be able to fight on for several days or weeks with little support from heavy weapons – tanks and artillery – or regular re-supply.

Since the first large scale parachute and glider landing operations in 1940, airborne troops of many nations have established a fearsome reputation for fighting spirit, tactical innovation and daring leadership. These traditions have now passed to troops and units who fly into battle largely by helicopter to fight the airborne battles of the 21st century.

Being an airborne warrior is also a state of mind. By their very nature airborne operations are prone to going wrong. The weather often throws parachute drops off course and paratroopers can land far from their intended landing zone. Planes or helicopters break down at the wrong moment. Paratroopers get injured on landing. Then the enemy can interfere by shooting down

in-bound aircraft or reinforcing their defences at the last minute. If something can go wrong, then it invariably will. Successful airborne operations are nearly always characterised by plans going wrong and airborne forces improvising to pull victory from the jaws of defeat. The history of airborne operations is littered with failures or victories that have resulted in enormous costs in lost lives, destroyed aircraft and abandoned equipment.

To overcome these challenges requires what is euphemistically termed 'airborne initiative' or 'the will to win'. The ability to 'adapt, improvise and overcome' in the face of overwhelming odds is what being an airborne soldier is all about. Troops who need detailed orders and perfectly organised supply lines to fight are not really made to serve in the airborne forces.

In *Airborne* we tell the story of some of the most important airborne operations over the past century. The first use of parachutes in combat can be traced back to August 1918 when an Italian officer, Alessandro Tandura, jumped behind Austro-Hungarian lines near Vittorio Veneto in a bid to collect intelligence on enemy positions. The Savoia-Pomilio SP.4 aircraft he jumped from was piloted by two British Royal Air Force officers, including one who would later father the Labour cabinet minister Tony Benn.

It is not recorded how successful Tandura's mission was but within a few years many armies and air forces were experimenting with large scale parachute drops by troops trained to seize key objectives behind enemy lines. World War Two saw huge battles involving thousands of airborne troops. Crete, D-Day in Normandy, and Arnhem are now iconic airborne battles. Since 1945 airborne forces have earned further glory. French paratroopers fought to their last rounds at Dien Ben Phu in 1954. British Royal Marines flew ashore by helicopter for the first time during the 1956 Suez conflict and opened the era of air mobility. The US Army's 'Air Cav' perfected the tactics of helicopter-borne air assault during the Vietnam conflict in the 1960s.

More recent conflicts in Iraq, Afghanistan and Ukraine have seen modern day airborne and air mobile forces face new threats and challenges on 21st century battlefields. US Army Rangers were some of the first American 'boots on the ground' in Afghanistan after their high profile parachute drop in the country in October 2001. While the US Army's

ABOVE: A CH-47 Chinook prepares to lift British and Japanese troops during an air mobility exercise in 2022. The twin rotor machine is the helicopter of choice for many nation's air assault forces. (MOD/CROWN COPYRIGHT)

LEFT: Fighting through the objective. A member of the British Army's 3rd Battalion, The Parachute Regiment during an urban warfare exercise. (MOD/CROWN COPYRIGHT)

BELOW: To the rally point. Once safely on the ground airborne forces have to rapidly organise to press on to seize their objectives before the enemy has time to mount an effective defence. (US DOD)

173rd Airborne Brigade combat jump into Iraq in March 2003 showed the strategic reach of America's airborne forces.

We hope *Airborne* does justice to the heroism of the airborne troops from around the world and provides insights into the success and failure of airborne operations. Not every airborne operation is recorded, but we have looked at the most important ones over the 80 years. The story of these battles is remarkable. All the forces we look at – from Britain, France, Germany, Poland, Russia, and the United States – shared a common ethos. It is about being willing to step out of an aircraft - or helicopter - into the unknown and then trying to snatch victory with whatever weapons and equipment they have to hand. The motto of the Special Air Service Regiment- one of the first British airborne units formed in World War Two – summed it up well, 'Who Dares Wins'.

Tim Ripley
February 2023

By Air to Battle

Airborne Forces and Tactics

RIGHT: Airborne forces have strategic reach, allowing them to launch from airbases in friendly territory and drop on targets deep inside enemy-held territory. (MOD/CROWN COPYRIGHT)

BELOW: Putting down paratroopers in a tight group prevents dispersal and reduces the time it takes for airborne units to rally and form up to take the fight to the enemy. (MOD/CROWN COPYRIGHT)

Modern airborne forces boast equipment that is far in advance of that used in action by their forefathers of World War Two. The fielding of modern transport helicopters in the 1960s transformed many aspects of airborne operations but the essential elements of what constitutes a successful mission have remained the same.

By necessity, airborne forces are very lightly armed, have limited heavy equipment and logistic support. They are at their most vulnerable when in the air or landing. Once on the ground,

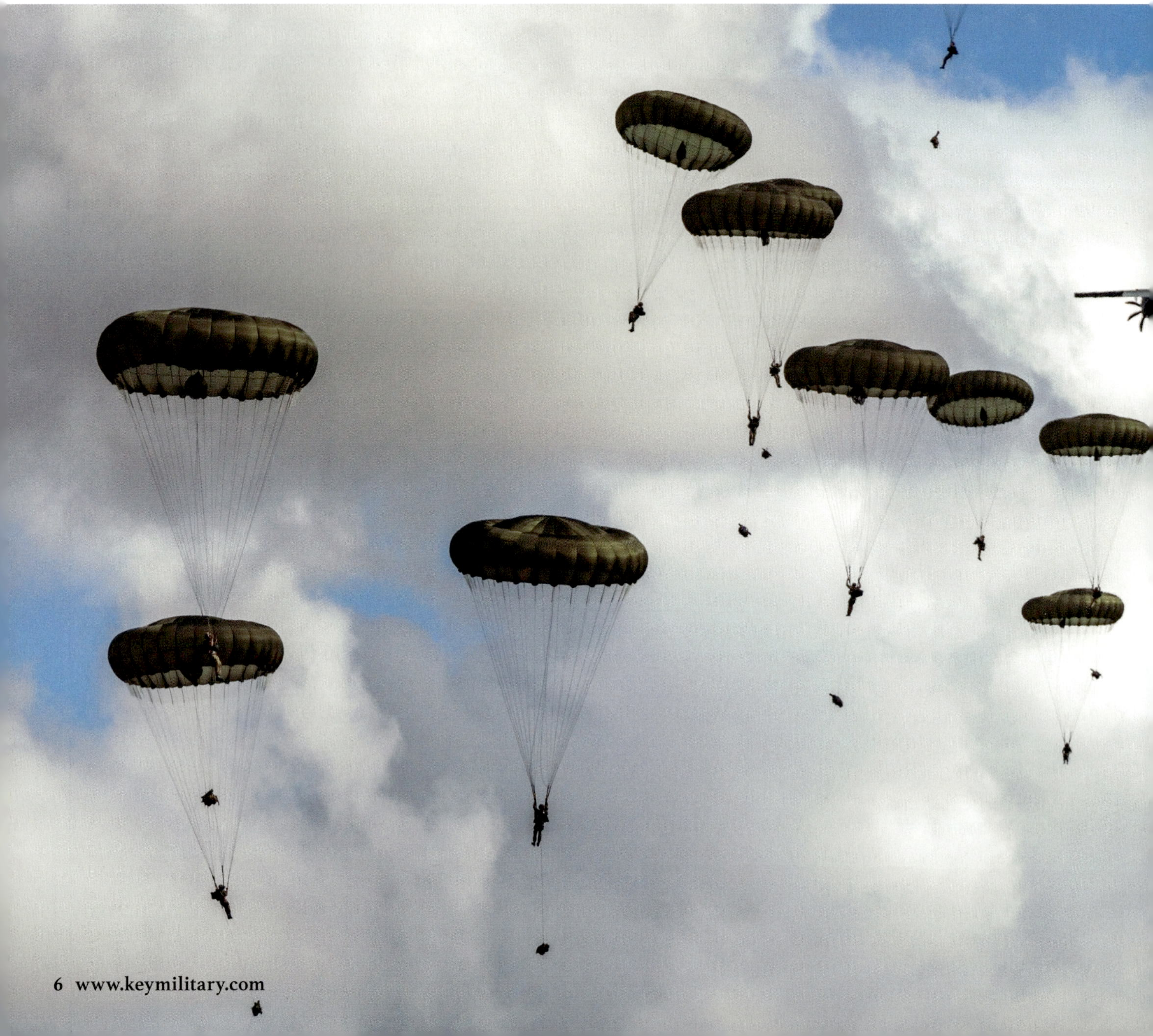

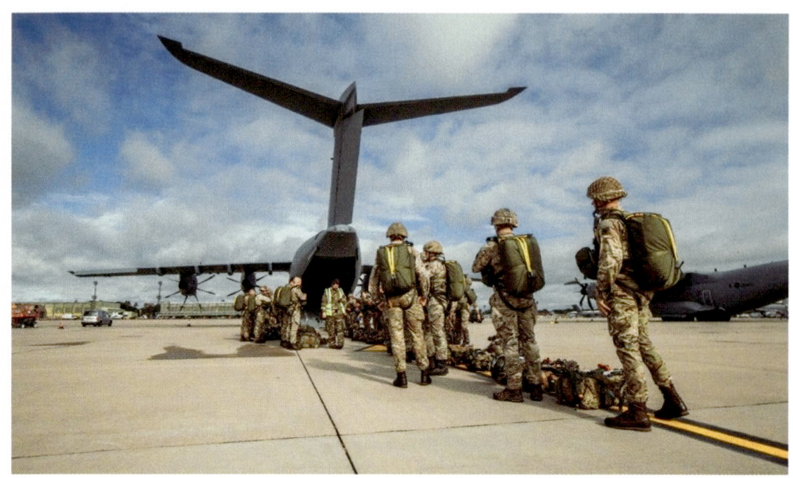

they have limited mobility and protection from enemy fire. So, to be successful, airborne troops have to be launched against an ill prepared enemy who is not expecting to come under attack. Surprise is the key to victory in airborne operations. By exploiting the enemy's momentary confusion, airborne troops can seize their objectives with little loss. The flipside is that any success needs to be rapidly reinforced or the lightly armed and protected airborne troops will be dislodged or destroyed by counter attacks. Time and again, airborne operations have gone wrong when relief forces have not been able to advance to link up with the advance wave.

Airborne operations can be launched to achieve a spread of objectives, from small scale tactical missions involving a few dozen troops to large operations intended to achieve decisive victory or strategic effect.

The execution of airborne operations using parachute, glider ➲

ABOVE: Jump masters are responsible for getting paratroopers out of aircraft as quickly as possible to reduce dispersal and vulnerability to enemy fire. (MOD/CROWN COPYRIGHT)

BELOW: US Army Rangers prepare to board a CH-47 Chinook ahead of an air assault operation in Afghanistan. (US DOD)

or helicopter landed forces is a complex and difficult business. While technology may have changed the tactics, techniques and procedures of airborne operations have not changed much over the decades.

Landing by parachute is inherently risky. Paratroopers can be blown off course or suffer injury on landing. Similarly, supplies, vehicles or heavy equipment dropped by parachute can be damaged on impact. Dispersal of paratroopers can be avoided by dropping paratroopers at very low level to limit their time in the air and reduce the risk of them being blown off course. Low level drops also reduce the chance of paratroopers being shot at from the ground, but they increase the risk of injury from heavy landings and often make it impossible to use reserve chutes if a paratrooper's main chute fails.

Many of these problems can be mitigated by selecting flat drop zones, which are away from forests, marshes or built up areas so paratrooper units can land and then re-organise themselves in a deliberate way, before setting off to seize their objectives. Often such ideal terrain is not located close to the assault unit's objectives. Airborne commanders, therefore, have to make a judgement on whether it is better to land close to their objectives and suffer higher losses from accidents and enemy fire or land further away, on better terrain, but risk losing the element of surprise.

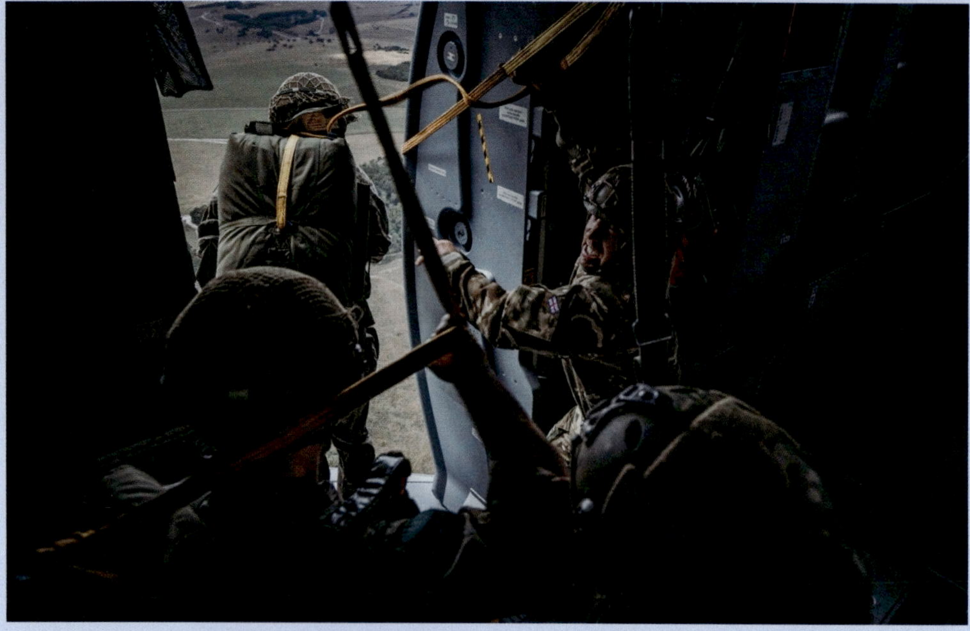

High Risk

For high risk but big pay off missions, airborne commanders can choose to land their troops directly onto enemy positions. These 'coup d'main' assaults often involve small groups of troops landing in the heart of the enemy defences. By their very nature, these missions are either dramatic successes or end with almost all the assault force being killed, wounded, or captured.

When planning larger operations, airborne commanders have to consider how to bring in reinforcements, large equipment, and supplies. In World War Two airborne forces relied on gliders to bring in heavier ordnance but they needed very specific conditions to operate safely. Finding suitable landing zones for gliders was a major issue in planning airborne missions in World War Two.

Another way to reinforce and resupply airborne forces is by seizing and using airfields to allow follow-up waves of reinforcements. Transport aircraft have seen their performance and load carrying capacity dramatically improve since the 1940s. When a World War Two era Douglas C-47 Dakota is compared to Boeing C-17 Globemaster it is possible to see how 21st century air landing operations are dramatically different in terms of their scale and size.

The advent of rugged and reliable helicopters in the 1960s transformed airborne operations. At a stroke, helicopters took away much of the uncertainty and risk involved in parachute

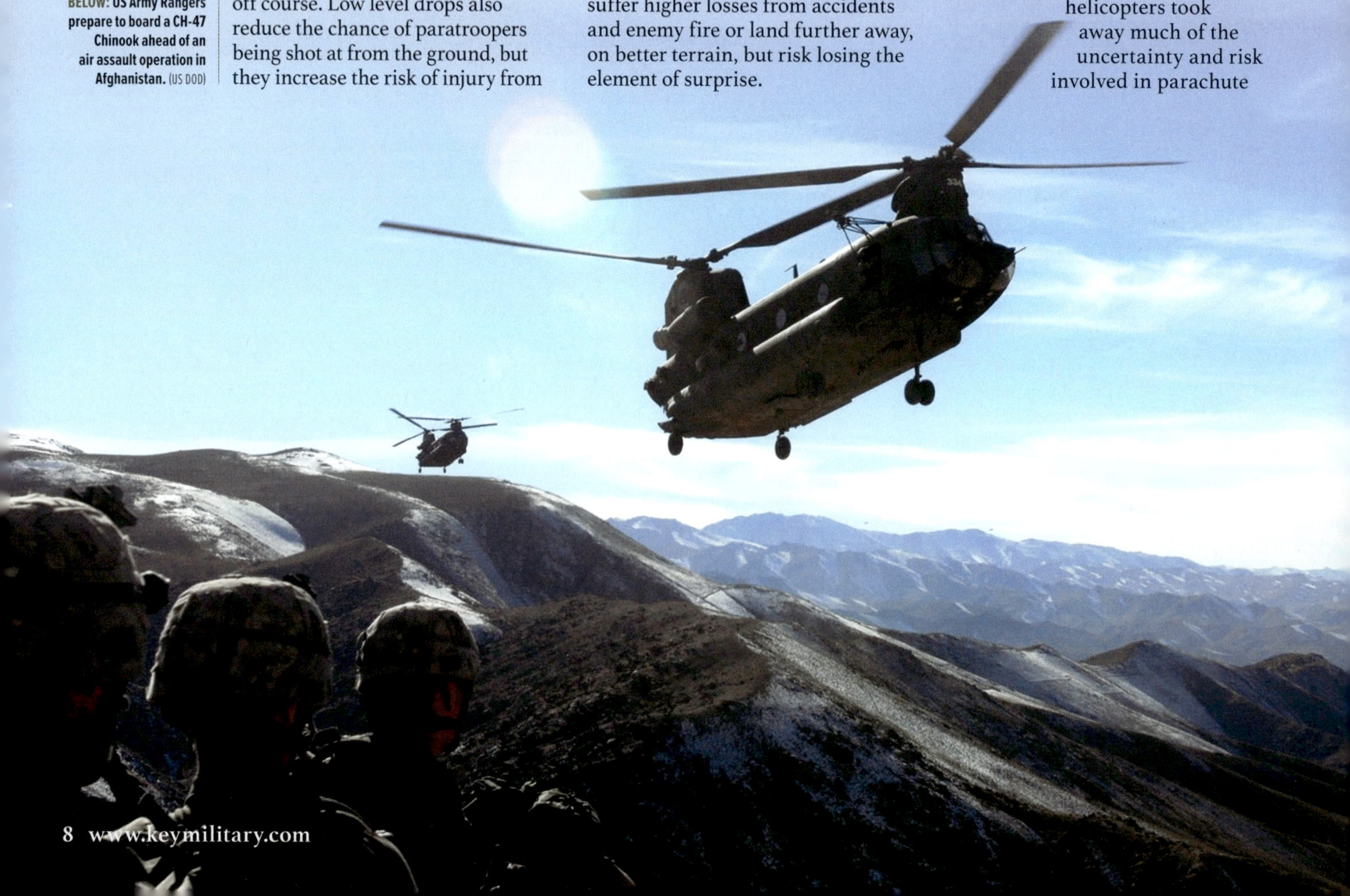

landings. Helicopters can deliver large numbers of troops with pinpoint accuracy without the risk of them breaking limbs on landing.

However, helicopters have their own limitations that have not totally rendered the paratrooper obsolete. Helicopters are noisy so the enemy can hear them coming and they are very vulnerable when they land or hover to unload their passengers. Commanders, therefore, have to plan helicopter routes very carefully to preserve the element of surprise and avoid enemy air defences.

Not all helicopters are capable of air-to-air refuelling, so they have limited range and endurance. This in effect limits the potential to use helicopters in strategic missions, far from friendly held territory. It is possible to carry out long range helicopter insertion missions, but it requires considerable planning to pre-position refuelling points along approach routes. Large transport helicopters can be equipped with extra fuel tanks or under slung fuel bladders to allow smaller helicopters to top up their tanks at improvised refuelling points.

Surprise

The limitations on using helicopters for long range missions means that the day of the parachute assault is not yet over. Parachuting still offers the best way to silently insert troops to seize strategic objectives deep behind enemy lines, to take the defenders by surprise. The ability to do this across thousands of miles distance offers decision makers many strategic options. The few nations that have ambitions for global power projection have all retained strong forces of paratroopers and their supporting transport aircraft to enable airborne troops to mount strategic operations at very short notice.

Although the advent of helicopters has taken away much of the risk involved in delivery by parachute, it has not meant that airborne troops have been able to water down their training and military ethos. The same 'airborne initiative' and 'can do' spirit of airborne forces is still very valuable in helicopter assault operations, which are also very prone to go wrong. If in the heat of battle enemy action limits the ability of helicopters to bring in reinforcements or supplies then the airborne troops will be on their own deep inside enemy territory. This is where the fighting spirit and ability to think on their feet in extreme situations is the key to victory.

Airborne warriors of the 21st century are equipped to a degree that their counterparts in World War Two would be envious. However, the experience modern paratroopers have when jumping out of an aircraft is essentially similar to that in the 1940s. The ground approaches just as fast and broken ankles or legs are just as painful.

The airborne spirit is proving to be just as valuable on the battle fields of this age as it was in the muddy fields of Normandy or the olives groves of Crete.

ABOVE: In the 1950s and 1960s airborne units became known as battlefield 'fire brigades' and were routinely dispatched to fight in so-called 'bushfire wars'. The British Parachute Regiment played a prominent role in the Aden conflict of the 1960s. (MOD/CROWN COPYRIGHT)

LEFT: The famous stretcher race is key part of the 'P-Company' training course to select future members of the British Airborne Force. (MOD/CROWN COPYRIGHT)

Hunters from the Sky

The Birth of Nazi Germany's Airborne Forces

RIGHT: Germany's Fallschirmjäger were formed as the elite strike force of the Nazi Luftwaffe in the run up to World War Two.
(AIRSEALAND PHOTOS)

Within days of coming to power in 1933 Adolf Hitler set in motion secret plans to shake off the shackles of the Versailles Treaty and begin German re-armament. The post World War One treaty prohibited Germany from operating military aircraft and other offensive weapons.

As part of his drive to build up German military power the Nazi leader gave orders to rebuild the country's air capability. He entrusted rebuilding the Luftwaffe to his trusted disciple Herman Göring, who had been a fighter ace in World War One. Hitler and Göring were convinced that paratroops and air landing forces could play an important part in their plans for high tempo offensive operations, or Blitzkrieg.

In the 1920s and 1930s the development of aircraft technology had accelerated at a rapid pace and by the time the Nazis were expanding Germany's military reliable large transport aircraft were in production. Experiments with parachutes were also well underway and many armed forces saw the potential of using the new airlift capabilities to deliver troops far behind enemy lines to either destroy or seize targets in surprise attacks. The Soviet Red Army formed the first large parachute units in the early 1930s and invited foreign observers, including Göring, to watch their exercises.

Göring was determined to accelerate the formation of Germany's airborne forces. In 1935 he ordered the Luftwaffe to form its first experimental parachute battalion. A jump school was opened at Spandau, outside Berlin. At the same time the German army formed its own parachute unit. Orders were placed for the Junkers Ju 52 tri-motor transport aircraft and this rugged design became the stalwart of German airborne operations in World War Two, with nearly 5,000 being built. German airborne pioneers were also very keen on using gliders to deliver troops silently into enemy territory and the DFS 230 glider, capable of carrying 10 soldiers was soon in service.

By 1938 Hitler was impressed with the progress of the first paratroop

units that he ordered another expansion. Dubbed Fallschirmjäger, which combined the German name for parachutes with the term for elite light infantry or hunters. They were soon known as the Hunters from the Sky.

The 7th Air Division was now formed to combine both the air force and army parachute units and this

BELOW: In the years before World War Two, German airborne commanders perfected the tactics of dropping large numbers of Fallschirmjäger from Ju 52 transports.
(AIRSEALAND PHOTOS)

ABOVE: The Ju 52 was the mainstay of the German airborne forces. It proved to be a rugged aircraft that could take plenty of enemy fire and keep flying. (WOLVENHEART)

unit was placed under Luftwaffe command. Its first commander was Major General Kurt Student, and he soon became known as the 'father of German airborne forces'. He accelerated the training of paratroopers, developing new tactics and specialist equipment for airborne warfare, such as parachute dropped supply containers, distinctive combat smocks and safety helmets.

As well as boosting the number and training of paratroopers and glider-borne troops, Student also pushed the German army to set up a dedicated air-landing unit that would be flown into airfields captured by the first wave of parachute drops. The 22nd Air Landing Division was assigned to work alongside the 7th Air Division in the Blitzkrieg battles of 1940.

The first recorded German parachute operation took place in March 1938, when a company was dropped to seize an airport outside Vienna during the unopposed Nazi invasion of Austria. When German troops invaded Poland in September 1939, Hitler deliberately kept his newly formed airborne troops out of the action. He wanted to keep the capabilities of German parachute units secret and left the job of finishing off the poorly armed Poles to his armoured or panzer divisions. When Student's airborne forces were unleashed against Western Europe in the spring of 1940 they would take the allies completely by surprise.

LEFT: Major General Kurt Student was dubbed the 'father of the German airborne forces' for his role in forming the first Fallschirmjäger units. (BUNDESARCHIV)

Blitzkrieg

Airborne Assaults against Western Europe 1940

ABOVE: German paratroops drop on Holland in the opening hours of the Nazi offensive to capture the country's key strategic government buildings and transport infra-structure. (FOTOCOLLECTIE SPAARNESTAD)

The first nation to spot the potential of using aviation to deliver troops on daring behind the lines missions to achieve decisive impact was Nazi Germany. After the defeat of Poland, Adolf Hitler ordered his military chiefs to develop plans to rapidly defeat the western allies in a series of Blitzkrieg strikes.

Hitler's first targets were neutral Denmark and Norway. He wanted to secure transit routes for the import of iron ore from Sweden and pre-empt any attempt by the British to set up naval and air bases in Norway.

Operation Weserübung envisaged simultaneous invasions of Denmark and Norway by air, land, and sea. Airborne troops spearheaded both attacks. German troops made the first every combat parachute drops in military history during the early hours of April 9 to capture Aalborg airfield and the Storstrøm Bridge in northern Denmark. They met no resistance. The Danish government soon ordered its army not to resist the German forces and there were minimal losses among the invasion force.

As German troops were surging into Denmark, an air and naval force was heading towards the Norwegian capital Oslo. The Germans had hoped to take the Norwegians by surprise, but their coastal batteries spotted a German cruiser leading the invasion flotilla south of the capital and opened fire, sinking the ship.

German air landing troops put down unopposed in a flotilla of Ju-52s at Oslo's Fornebu airport and then headed into the city after dawn. Other air landing troops seized Kristiansand airport at Kjevik but a company of 132 paratroopers who jumped onto Sola Air Station, near Stavanger, met resistance and three of the attackers were killed. This was the first ever opposed parachute landing.

RIGHT: Norway's capital Oslo fell to air landed German troops on April 9, 1940. (HENRIKSEN & STEEN)

The delay in capturing Oslo allowed the Norwegian King and his government to escape from the capital and head north. A race now developed between the Germans and the allies – Britain and France – to seize key ports and airbases along Norway's long coastline.

A German naval force headed for Narvik in the far north of Norway to put a landing force ashore. A parachute company was then dropped on the town, which surrendered to the German forces on April 9. German troops were eventually forced to retreat after British and French troops landed in a counter move.

Further south, other German forces were moving in hot pursuit of the retreating Norwegians. In a bid to cut off the Norwegian retreat a company of 150 paratroopers was dropped at the railway junction at Bjørnfjell. However, they were soon surrounded and suffered more than 100 losses until a ground column relieved them five days later.

The Norwegian campaign dragged on into June, until the British and French ordered their troops to be evacuated from the Narvik area. The limited airborne and air landing operations had given the German paratroops their first combat experience, but they had not been decisive to the outcome of the campaign. The next German operations would be far more ambitious.

Operation Grey

Hitler approved a daring plan, code-named Operation Grey, to defeat France by splitting its armies in half using a panzer advance through the Ardennes region. To confuse the Allied high command a German offensive would first sweep into Holland and Belgium. This would prompt the British and French armies to enter Belgium to help hold the Germans back. Just at this moment, panzer columns would strike the thinly defended Ardennes – in the ➤

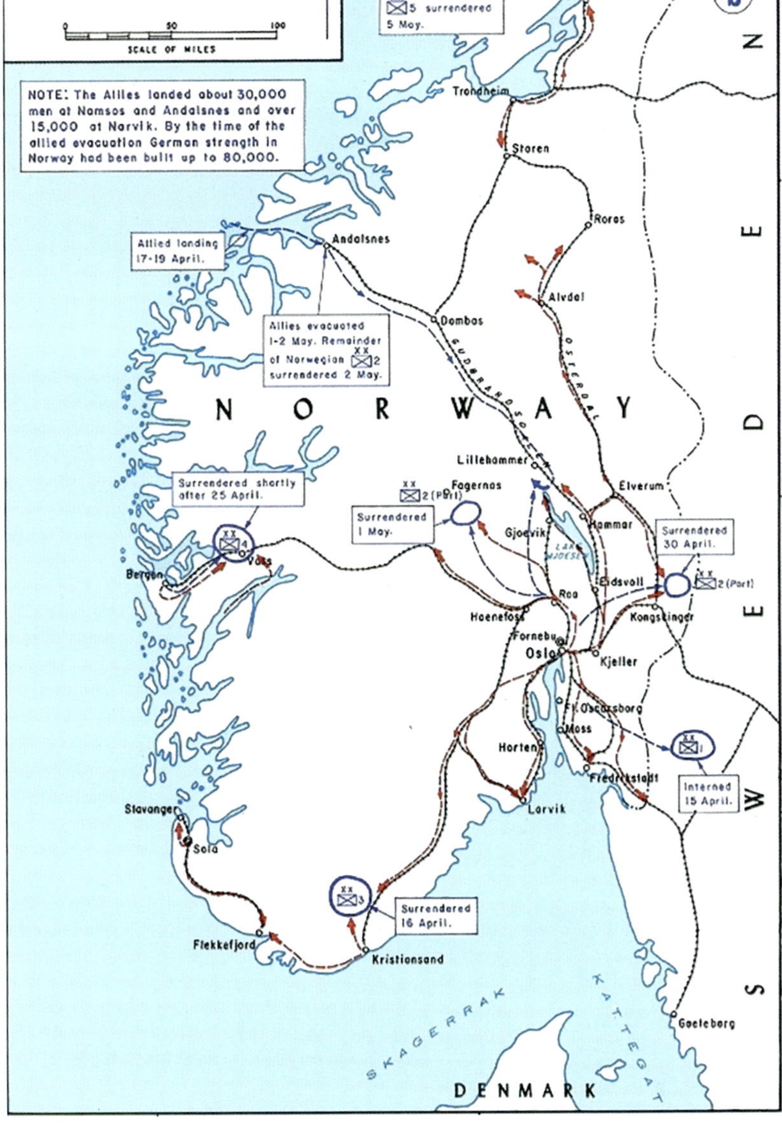

south of Belgium - and begin their encircling move. The Allies' best troops would be cut off and destroyed in northern France and Belgium. To encourage the Allies take the bait, the German advance into Holland and central Belgium had to be made to look like Hitler's main effort. This is where Kurt Student's airborne forces came into play.

The Dutch and Belgians had built a series of defensive lines along key canals and rivers. To overcome these defences, Student proposed landing airborne troops to seize key bridges in a series of surprise landings. In an added twist, Student also planned to land a strong force at airfields outside the Dutch capital, The Hague, and then make a rapid advance into the city to seize the country's government and royal family. Operation Fortress was a daring plan and nothing like it had ever been attempted before.

Operation Fortress got underway on May 10, with German air forces striking hard at targets in Holland, Belgium, and France. Behind the first wave of bombers heading into Dutch airspace were hundreds of Ju 52s carrying Student's paratroopers.

A battalion of paratroopers were dropped on airfields at Ypenburg, Ockenburg, and Valkenburg outside the Dutch capital and the took the defenders by surprise. The plan was for units of the 22nd Air Landing Division to fly in soon afterwards. However, Dutch army units quickly counter attacked and penned the Germans into small enclaves. At Ockenburg and Valkenburg the Dutch defenders destroyed Ju 52s trying to land reinforcements and blocked the runway, preventing further German troops being flown in. Only at Ypenburg did the Germans control the

runway. However, it was not finished, and the completed concrete surface was not long enough to allow Ju 52s to take off. German aircraft tried to land on a nearby beach but were destroyed by gun fire from a Dutch frigate. By the end of the day, more Dutch troops had arrived and pushed the German off the airfields. The surviving paratroopers went to ground in woods and tried to hold out until German ground troops arrived. Student's coup d'main against the Dutch government had failed. Nearly 1,600 German paratroopers and air landing soldiers were captured in the fighting and some 400 were killed. The heavy Dutch fire on the airfields destroyed or damaged 182 Ju 52s.

Further south, the bulk of Student's forces were committed to capture the city of Rotterdam and key bridges over the Neder Rijn, Waal and Maas rivers to open strategic routes for German ground troops. These operations met more success than their comrades did in The Hague.

One battalion of paratroopers landed on each side of the key bridge at Moerdijk over the Maas and quickly captured it with few losses. Two platoons of paratroops also seized the bridge over the Waal at Dordrecht but were soon locked in a bitter fight with Dutch troops and eventually had to withdraw. In the centre of Rotterdam, a platoon of paratroopers dropped on the north bank of the Neder Rijn to capture a strategic bridge. At the same time 12 German sea planes landed on the river and delivered 100 troops to storm the southern end of

the bridge. Just to the south of the city, Student dropped a battalion of paratroopers on Waalhaven airfield as a bridgehead to allow follow up waves of troops to be flown in to reinforce his troops. They quickly drove off the defenders and Student arrived to take command of the operation.

In an added twist, units of the German intelligence service's commando unit, the Brandenberg Division, had infiltrated Holland the night before the invasion dressed in Dutch uniforms to carry out acts of sabotage or try to capture smaller bridges. Their activities, along with the German parachute drops, created panic and confusion in the Dutch military command. By now the main German ground force had started to advance rapidly west over the Dutch border and move to link up with their airborne units. The Dutch Royal Family left the country on a British Royal Navy warship on May 13 as resistance started to crumble.

Student's troops held out in their bridgeheads in Rotterdam for three days in the face of determined Dutch counter attacks until German tank columns managed to reach the beleaguered paratroopers. The Dutch defenders of the city continued to put up strong resistance. An all out attack was ordered for May 14 involving tanks and ground troops, backed by a huge Luftwaffe bombing attack.

German paratroops were to play a key role by launching an amphibious assault across the Neder Rijn.

Surrender

Ahead of the attack on May 14, the German high command issued a surrender ultimatum to the Dutch commander. After this was agreed, the German ground assault was called off, but the stop order did not reach 90 Luftwaffe bombers in time, and they flew on to devastate the city. The raid killed 900 civilians and flattened 24,500 homes, making 80,000 people homeless. As a result of the carnage the Dutch commander in the city surrendered to spare it from more attacks. Hours later the Dutch army command began negotiations to surrender the country and by early on May 15 it laid down its arms.

As the Germans were battling in Holland, to the south another German force was advancing towards Brussels, via the border city of Maastricht, to further confuse the Allied high command. Blocking the German advance was the wide Albert Canal that had been fortified with field defences. To capture the three bridges over the canal and Fort Eben Emael, which had gun turrets that dominated possible crossing points, Student formed a 400-strong special attack unit, known as Assault Detachment Koch. It was ⊘

ABOVE: German paratroops aimed to seize the Dutch capital on May 10, 1940, and decapitate the country's political and military leadership. (DUTCH NATIONAL ARCHIVES)

LEFT: The Dutch military had built a series of defensive lines to stop invading forces from crossing the country's many rivers and canals. In many cases the airborne troops simply bypassed them. (NIELS BOSBOOM)

BELOW: Dutch troops secure concrete defences on Nijmegen bridge ahead of the arrival of German tank columns. (BUNDESARCHIV)

RIGHT: German paratroopers landing at Ockenburg airstrip near The Hague, in their failed attempt to capture the Dutch capital. (NIOD INSTITUUT VOOR OORLOGS-, HOLOCAUST- EN GENOCIDESTUDIES)

BELOW: The ruins of Rotterdam after the German terror bombing that devastated the city. (US DEFENSE VISUAL INFORMATION CENTER)

ordered to capture the three bridges and Fort Eben Emael in a co-ordinated series of surprise glider attacks.

Just before dawn on May 10, 32 DFS 230 gliders landed close to their objectives and the assault troops swung into action. Two of the assault teams managed to reach their objectives and removed the demolition charges, preventing the defenders blowing the bridges up. On the third bridge, the defenders managed to detonate the charges and bring it down. At all the bridges the German airborne troops were soon locked in bitter fighting with Belgian troops until early afternoon when panzer columns arrived to relieve them.

The most important success came when 85 Germans landed in a further nine DFS 230 gliders on the roof of

Fort Eben Emael, which dominated the strategic bridges over the Albert Canal. The silent dawn approach of the gliders meant the defenders did not realise they were under attack until they heard Germans attaching explosive charges to their gun turrets.

Eben Emael fort was designed to use its guns to devastate attackers massing to cross the Albert Canal, and they could not be depressed to engage the Germans already on and around the fort. Systematically, the Germans worked their way through all the gun turrets, blowing them one by one. The attack was such a surprise that by

the time the Belgians had organised enough to counter attack, the fort was effectively out of action and German assault troops had seized the canal bridges. Almost 1,000 Belgian troops eventually surrendered to the German paratroopers. It was next stop Brussels for the German Blitzkrieg.

The assault on Eben Emael was a classic coup d'main that maximised surprise and new weapons to achieve victory over more numerous enemies. By using near silent gliders, the Fallschirmjäger made innovative use of aircraft to deliver elite troops to their target.

ABOVE: The Belgian fortress at Eben Emael dominated strategic crossings over the Meuse river with its armoured turret fitted with 75mm rapid-fire guns. (WASILY)

BELOW: German DFS 230 gliders delivered the assault force silently onto the roof of the Eben-Emael fortress. (BRITISH AIR MINISTRY)

Operation Mercury

The Airborne Invasion of Crete, May 1941

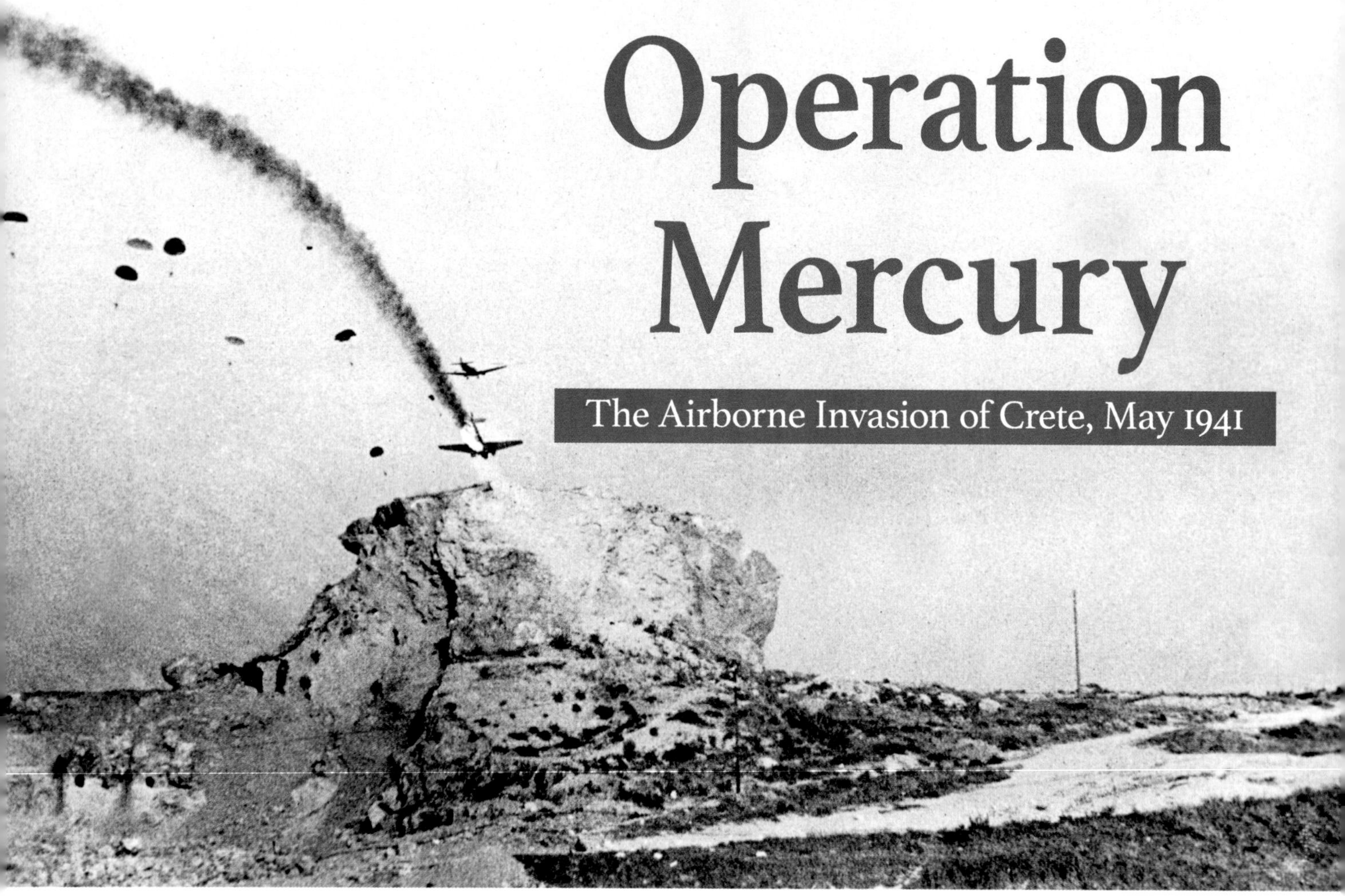

ABOVE: A Ju 52 on fire during the German air assault on Heraklion. (AIRSEALAND PHOTOS)

In the final days of April 1941, the last British troops were evacuated from mainland Greece. German panzer columns had driven into Athens a few days before to complete Adolf Hitler's Blitzkrieg conquest of mainland Europe.

British Empire and Free Greek forces remained on the island of Crete, nearly 200 kilometres out into the Mediterranean. Hitler's attention was now shifting east, and he was in the process of massing his troops ready for Operation Barbarossa, the invasion of the Soviet Union. From Crete British bombers could potentially strike at Romanian oil fields and Hitler was determined to neutralise this threat before he turned his attentions to Russia.

Lieutenant General Kurt Student was given the mission of taking Crete with his airborne forces. This was to be the first time an island would be captured using only airborne troops and air support.

On April 20 - even before British troops had been driven from Greece – Hitler had ordered Student's XI Air Corps to begin massing around seven airfields in central Greece for Operation Mercury. Student had 25,000 troops available, including paratroopers of the 7th Air Division

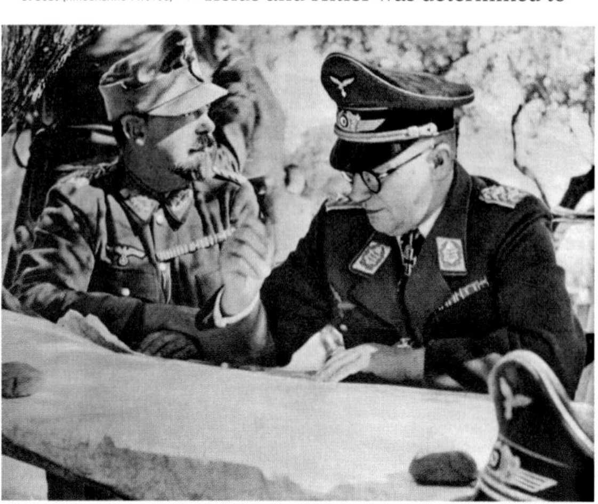

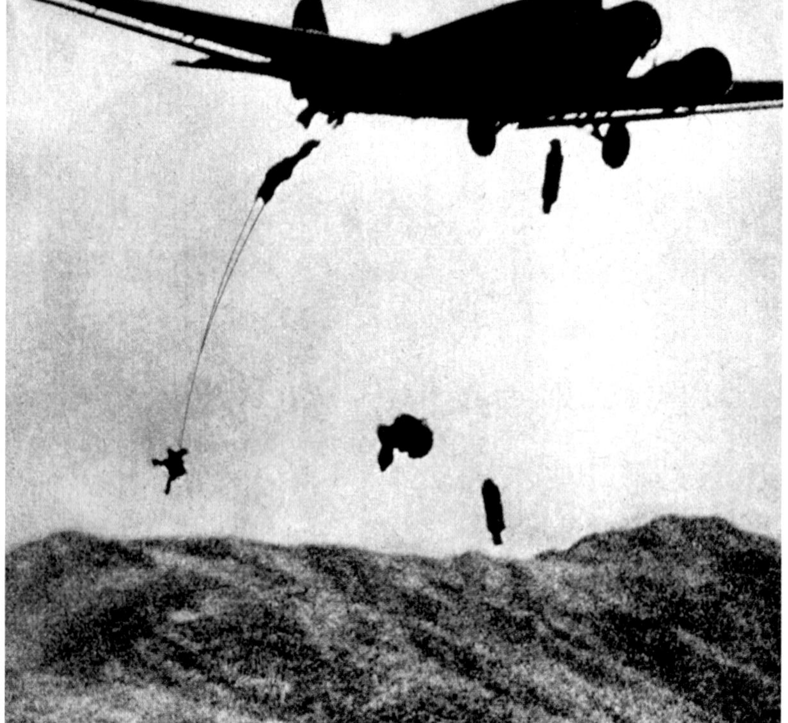

RIGHT: German aircraft flew ultra low over their drop zones in a bid reduce the time the Fallschirmjäger had to spend in the air. (AIRSEALAND PHOTOS)

BELOW: Lieutenant General Kurt Student masterminded the German air assault on Crete. (AIRSEALAND PHOTOS)

and mountain troops of the 6th
Mountain Division, operating in the
air landing role. The force would be
carried into battle in 500 Junkers Ju
52 transport aircraft and 80 DFS 230
gliders.

The VIII Air Corps of General
Wolfram Freiherr von Richthofen –
cousin of the famous World War
One Red Baron – was assigned to
help Student, with its 150 Ju 87 Stuka
dive bombers, 120 Dorner Do 17 and
40 Heinkel He 111 bombers, and 90
Messerschmitt Me 109 and Me 110
fighters. Their job was to win and
keep air supremacy over Crete.

Defending Crete were 27,500
British Empire troops, including
strong Australian and New Zealand
contingents, as well as 14,000 Greek
troops and militia fighters. Most
of these had been evacuated from
Greece only weeks before with little
more than their personal weapons.
They had only a couple of dozen
artillery pieces, few anti-aircraft
guns and eight light tanks, as well
as limited ammunition and little

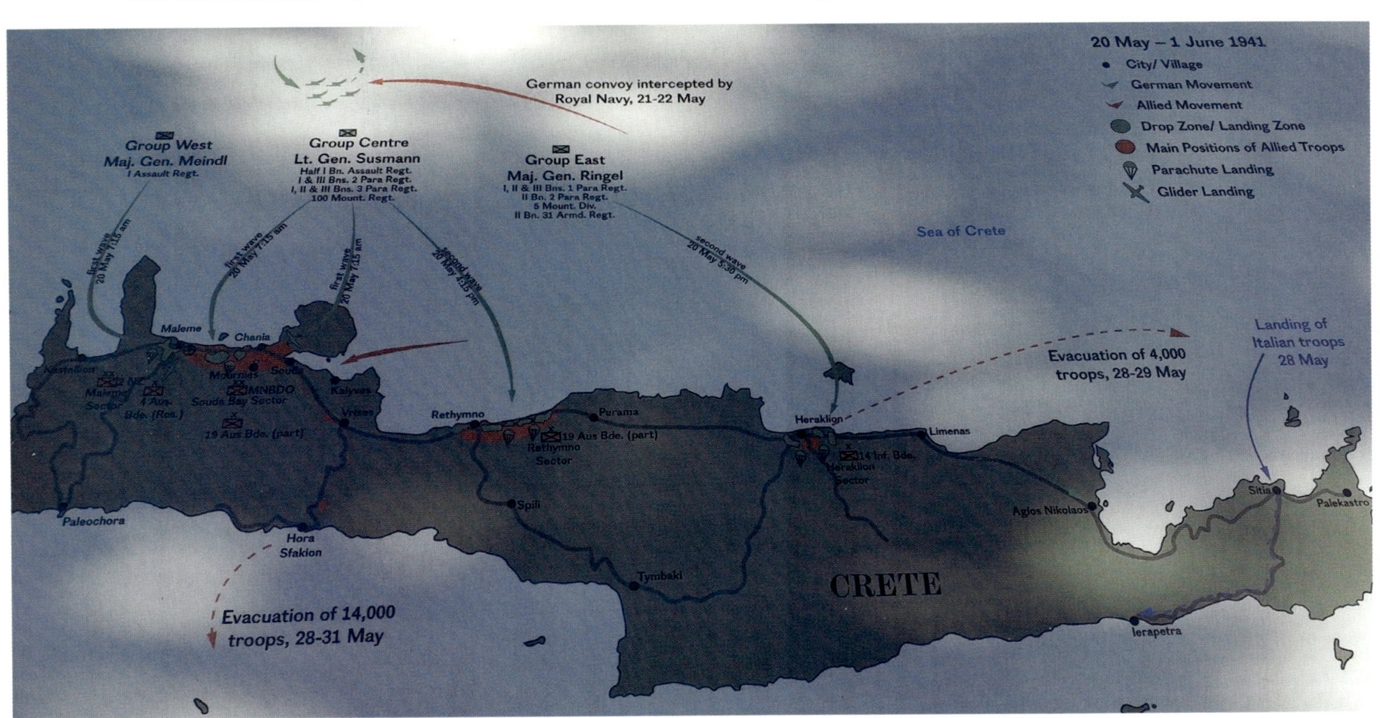

fuel for their motor transport. What the force lacked in materiel they made up for in fighting spirit. Their commander, New Zealander Major General Bernard Freyberg, was a bulldog warrior who had won the Victoria Cross in World War One. He was determined to give the Germans a fight when they tried to take the island. While the Royal Navy was able to keep open vital supply lines to British bases in Egypt, the Royal Air Force could only spare 36 Hawker Hurricane and Gloucester Gladiator fighters to defend Crete. Far from being a launch pad for RAF bombers, Crete was more of a beleaguered outpost.

Key Airfields

Student's plan to take Crete involved two waves of paratroopers landing to seize the island's three major airfields, at Maleme in the east, Retimo in the centre and Heraklion in the east, as well as the island's capital at Chania. Air landing troops would then follow up in waves of Ju 52s and they would fan out to capture ports along the north coast to welcome mountain troops sailing on a flotilla of commandeered Greek ships, escorted by Italian warships. The Germans expected the operation to be over in a matter of days.

Freyberg had been forewarned of the German plans thanks to the British Ultra code breaking organisation at Bletchley Park and had positioned his troops to defend the main airfields and landing beaches.

During the weeks before the German assault Richthofen's aircraft mounted a relentless bombardment of the island. Any troops or vehicles that broke cover were attacked by Stukas and in a bid to conserve his few anti-aircraft guns, Freyberg ordered them to hold their fire and remain camouflaged until the Ju 52s loaded with paratroopers appeared overhead. The defenders had to spend weeks hiding in trenches or living under cover in olive fields waiting for the German paratroopers to appear.

The Luftwaffe air offensive had destroyed all but a handful of the RAF fighters and on May 19, the last

aircraft were evacuated from Maleme to Egypt. The Germans planned to launch their first parachute landing the following day. British Prime Minister Winston Churchill signalled the allied supreme commander in Middle East, General Sir Archibald Wavell, warning him that the code breakers had picked up the German decision to attack, saying "it ought to be fine opportunity for the killing of the parachute troops."

Even though Student had mustered the largest ever concentration of Ju 52s, he still did not have enough to lift all his division in one go. The force was split into two waves, with the first landing around Maleme and Chania in the morning of May 20 and the second wave landing at Retimo and Heraklion in the afternoon.

The defending troops knew that something was different about the morning of May 20 when the air raids intensified and then appeared to suddenly stop. Then the waves of Ju 52s could be seen overhead, and the killing started.

Maleme airfield was the objective for a glider assault and a drop by the three battalions of Airborne Assault Regiment. The glider troops managed to land safely and capture the Tavronitis bridge at the southern edge of the airfield, but they were soon pinned down by New Zealand fire. One parachute battalion was

dropped on top of Hill 107, which overlooked the airfield and had been fortified by New Zealand troops. As the paratroopers drifted to earth, the defenders of the hill came out of their trenches and started to fire at the Germans. Hundreds were killed or wounded in a matter of minutes. The other two battalions landed to the west of Tavronitis bridge in undefended areas but high winds

scattered the paratroopers away from their drop zones, creating confusion and delaying their arrival on the key battlefield.

The assault force of the 3rd Parachute Regiment at Chania fared even worse after it was also dropped on top of more New Zealand positions. Its troops were isolated in small detachments that were soon locked in desperate battles with the ➲

RIGHT: German mountain troops formed the second wave of Operation Mercury and were flown by Ju 52s direct to Maleme airfield, which was still swept by allied artillery fire. (AIRSEALAND PHOTOS)

New Zealand defenders and Greek militia fighters.

In the afternoon Student launched his second wave and it soon ran into fierce resistance. The 2nd Parachute Regiment jumped around Retimo airfield and suffered heavy casualties as Australian and Greek troops machine gunned the descending paratroops.

There was even less success at Heraklion, where the 1st Parachute Regiment had the misfortune to be dropped on top of the Black Watch Highlanders and an Australian battalion. The two German companies that jumped nearest to the airfield were wiped out, with only five men escaping.

By the end of the first day, the Germans had failed to capture any of the airfields and the paratroopers that had landed were pinned down by determined resistance. However, overnight Student's desperate paratroopers at Maleme had a stroke of luck that turned the battle. The New Zealand commander controlling the defence of the airfield and Hill 107 lost contact with his forward troops inside the airfield. Fearing they had been overrun, he ordered the defenders of Hill 107 to pull back. The Germans could not believe their luck and early in the morning of May 21, they had taken the hill and then quickly swept into the airfield.

With a runway now under his control, Student ordered a Ju 52 loaded with mountain troops to make a test landing at Maleme. Despite the New Zealand troops firing every artillery piece and mortar they had at the aircraft as it approached, the Junkers got down safely and in a matter of seconds its passengers had jumped out, allowing the aircraft to take off. Once the technique had been proven, Student ordered more planes to follow.

By late afternoon, hundreds of reinforcements had been landed. New Zealand fire stilled raked the airfield and soon dozens of damaged and immobilised Junkers were strewn around the airfield, but Student ordered them to keep landing. Paratroopers commandeered an abandoned British tank to pull the wrecks off the runway to allow more planes to land. This was the strategy of reinforcing success. No more troops were sent to reinforce Chania, Retima, or Heraklion. The isolated pockets of paratroopers holding out in these areas would have to wait to be relieved.

Air Superiority

Freyberg soon realised the danger posed by the German lodgement at Maleme and ordered the New Zealand brigade in the area to launch immediate counter attacks to try to regain control of the airfield. Now, German control of the air proved decisive. The New Zealand troops could not move in the open in daylight and only had a few hours of night time to get their attack organised. By the time they attacked, the Germans were ready, and it soon broke down.

On May 21 and May 22, two German seaborne landing flotillas were intercepted by Royal Navy warships north of Crete and dispersed. More than 500 mountain troops were lost to British fire. Student's troops on Crete were now totally dependent on Maleme airfield for reinforcements and re-supply.

BELOW: German Fallschirmjäger faced their toughest test overcoming the allied defences on Crete. (AIRSEALAND PHOTOS)

By May 23, Student had enough troops and supplies on Crete to begin an offensive aimed at capturing Chania. The New Zealanders and Australians, aided by armed Greek civilians put up fanatical resistance but the momentum was now with the Germans. In heavy fighting on May 25 and 26, the Germans backed by their superior air power broke through the allied defence lines around Chania and the Souda Bay naval base. On May 27 Freyberg requested permission from Wavell to begin evacuating his troops from Crete. The British Empire troops broke contact with the Germans and began heading for the south coast to be picked up by the Royal Navy. The isolated garrisons defending Retimo and Heraklion were also ordered to head for safety. The brave Australians at Retimo did not receive the evacuation order in time and were captured when a German column approached their position. The last allied troops were picked up on the morning of May 31.

The battle for Crete had been bloody for both sides. Of the British Empire garrison, nearly 1,800 had been killed and 12,000 were eventually captured. Only 15,000 were safely evacuated. Several thousand Greek troops and civilians were killed in the fighting and in subsequent massacres by German troops.

Student and his paratroopers had won a great victory – the first time a battle had been fought entirely by air delivered forces. Nearly 10,000 Germans had dropped by parachute, 750 had landed by glider and 5,000 had been flown in by Ju 52s. Once the British retreat had been ordered a further 6,000 reinforcements had been able to land by sea.

The price of victory was horrendous. Out of the 22,000 German troops committed, more than 5,000 had been killed, including a quarter of the elite paratroopers. The Luftwaffe lost hundreds of aircraft, including 271 Junkers transports.

In the aftermath of the Crete offensive, Hitler was convinced that airborne operations were too costly, and he cancelled a proposed plan to capture the strategic island of Malta in the central Mediterranean in an airborne assault, telling a disappointed Student, that "the day of the parachutist is over." The German airborne general described Crete as "the graveyard of the German paratroopers."

ABOVE: General Student called Crete the 'graveyard of the German paratroopers' because of the heavy casualties they suffered. (BUNDESARCHIV)

BELOW: The German military graveyard at Maleme overlooks the airfield were so many Fallschirmjäger died in May 1941. (TIM RIPLEY)

Taking the Fight to Occupied Europe

Allied Airborne Forces

ABOVE: British airborne forces spearheaded the allied invasion of Vichy French controlled North Africa in the winter of 1942 in their first major campaign.
(IMPERIAL WAR MUSEUM)

The Royal Air Force provided a handful of Armstrong Whitworth Whitley bombers to allow the new airborne troops to practice parachuting. These surplus bombers were far from ideal for low level mass parachuting as the only safe way to exit the aircraft was through a small hatch in the floor of the rear fuselage.

It was not until February 1941 that the 11th SAS Battalion was sent into action to destroy a water supply aqueduct in southern Italy. Although the 36 men who took off from Malta in six Whitleys managed to safely land in Italy and successfully blow up their target, the attackers were all eventually captured as they attempted to reach the coast for a rendezvous with Royal Navy submarine.

Despite this setback, more troops and resources were soon assigned to the British airborne forces. In September 1941, the 11th SAS Battalion was renamed 1st Parachute Battalion and the following year the Parachute Regiment became a permanent unit of the British Army.

As the German Blitzkrieg swept across Europe in the early summer of 1940, it became obvious to Britain's political and military leaders that they would have to change the way they fought if the allies were to stand a chance of defeating Nazi military dominance.

Famously, on June 22, 1940 British Prime Minister Winston Churchill called for the formation of a corps of 5,000 parachute troops to take the fight to the Germans.

A few weeks earlier, the Air Ministry had set in motion the opening of a parachute training depot at Ringway airport south of Manchester, on the site of the city's now bustling international airport. One of the newly formed raiding units, No.2 Commando, was directed to Ringway to begin training to land by parachute. It was soon re-named the 11th Special Air Service (SAS) Battalion. This was a separate and distinct unit from L Detachment SAS formed in Egypt in 1941 by David Stirling. He went on to achieve fame for his desert raiding mission and is recognised as the founder of the modern day SAS.

The Red Devils

British military chiefs were convinced that airborne troops had a key role to play in supporting the

RIGHT: The PIAT gun provided British airborne forces with lightweight anti-tank firepower to take on German panzer counter-attacks.
(MOD/CROWN COPYRIGHT)

LEFT: The newly created British airborne forces had their first success at Bruneval in February 1942 when a raiding force seized a top secret German radar and successfully brought it back to Britain. (IMPERIAL WAR MUSEUM)

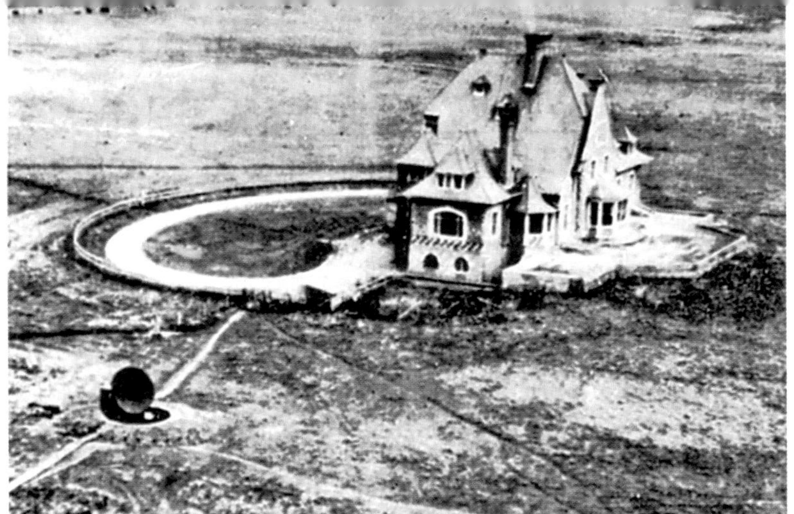

amphibious landing that would eventually be needed to wrestle control of Europe from the Nazis. Eventually 17 battalions of parachute troops would be formed by the British Army during the war. In 1941 the first British airborne division was formed under the command of Major General Frederick 'Boy' Browning. It took part in the Operation Torch landing in French North Africa towards the end of 1942. In July 1943, British and US parachute and glider-landed troops spearheaded the invasion of Sicily. This was the first large scale set piece airborne operation conducted in co-ordination with an Allied amphibious landing. The British and American air assault troops suffered heavy losses when parachutists and gliders were mistakenly put down in the Mediterranean Sea, but many lessons were learned, and improvements made in tactics and procedures ahead of the main allied invasion of France in 1944. The Germans took notice of their new opponents and soon dubbed them the 'Red Devils' on account of their ferocious bravery and distinctive maroon coloured berets. The British paratroopers soon adopted the nickname.

By the time of D-Day in June 1944, the British airborne forces had been grouped into the 1st Airborne Corps, which contained the two main fighting divisions, the 1st and 6th Airborne Divisions, and the SAS Brigade. The later formation contained British, Free French, and Belgian SAS units which were to land deep inside France and lead resistance groups attacking German lines of communications in the run up to the allied landings in Normandy. These French and Belgian SAS units are the forefathers of their country's modern day airborne forces.

Britain's airborne pioneers led the way in developing the tactics and procedures of air assault operations. A key British success was developing large gliders, Airspeed Horsas and the General Aircraft Hamilcar, which could

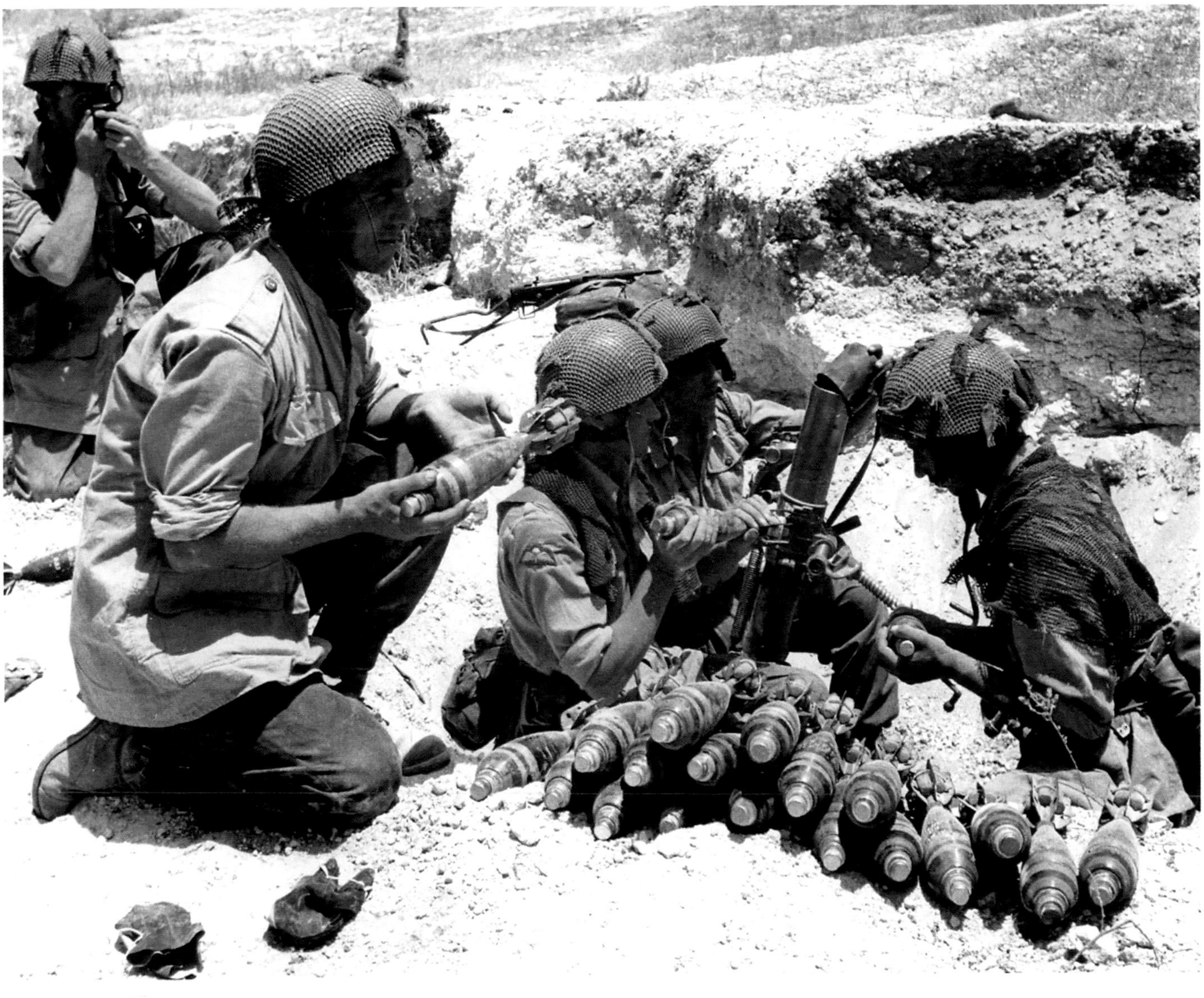

BELOW: British airborne forces only had light weapons, such as mortars, that they could carry in battle. (MOD/CROWN COPYRIGHT)

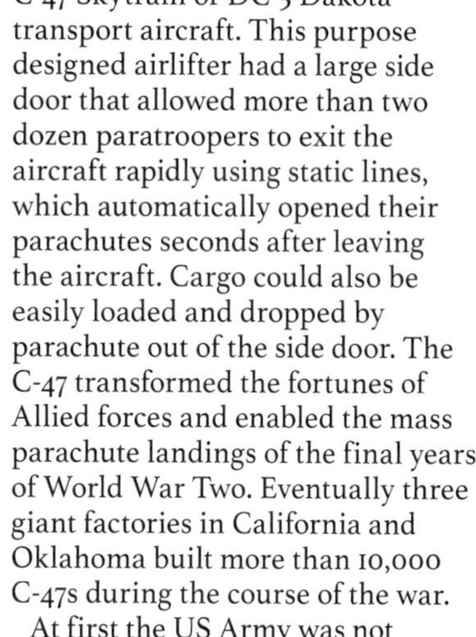

carry Jeeps, anti-tank guns and Tetrarch light tanks. These gave airborne units a small amount of tactical mobility and the ability to take on German panzers.

Over the Atlantic the US Army was watching events in Europe closely and ordered the formation of the first experimental parachute platoon in June 1940. The United States Army had a major advantage over its British counterpart. At this stage, the US Air Force had not been formed and the US Army Air Forces remained under the control of the US Army chain of command. As a result, the US Airborne Forces did not suffer from the shortage of airlift that plagued the development of Britain's airborne forces who had to rely on a rival service, the Royal Air Force for air transport.

The American aircraft industry also produced the iconic Douglas C-47 Skytrain or DC-3 Dakota transport aircraft. This purpose designed airlifter had a large side door that allowed more than two dozen paratroopers to exit the aircraft rapidly using static lines, which automatically opened their parachutes seconds after leaving the aircraft. Cargo could also be easily loaded and dropped by parachute out of the side door. The C-47 transformed the fortunes of Allied forces and enabled the mass parachute landings of the final years of World War Two. Eventually three giant factories in California and Oklahoma built more than 10,000 C-47s during the course of the war.

At first the US Army was not convinced that it needed large airborne divisions to conduct operations to seize and hold ground. It instead concentrated on building up parachute dropped raiding battalions and regiments. These saw action during Operation Torch. However, once senior US officers joined the British planning efforts for the invasion of Europe, they became convinced that large airborne formation were needed. In August 1942, the US Army's 82nd Division was converted into the first US Airborne Division. The 'All American' Division took part in the invasion of Sicily in July 1943 before moving to England, ahead of D-Day.

It was led during the key years of the war by Major Generals Matthew Taylor and James Gavin.

Band of Brothers

In England, the 82nd Airborne joined the 101st Airborne Division, which had been formed from scratch in August 1942. Known as the 'Screaming Eagles', the 101st Division would lead the allied advance from Normandy into Germany and its troopers were immortalised in the book and television series, *Band of Brothers*. The division was famously commanded during 1944 and 1945 by Major General Maxwell Taylor.

In the aftermath of D-Day, the British and Americans decided to combine their airborne forces into a powerful strike unit, dubbed the 1st Allied Airborne Army. This combined for the first time the two divisions of the British 1st Airborne Corps, with the two divisions of the US XVIII Airborne Corps and the aircraft of the USAAF's IX Troop Carrier Command, as well as troop carrying groups and squadrons of RAF Transport Command. A USAAF officer, Lieutenant General Lewis Brereton was appointed to command the airborne army when it was stood up on August 2, 1944.

This was the largest airborne force ever assembled and when it was unleashed against Holland in September 1944 it impressed the father of the German airborne forces, Colonel General Kurt Student. He had been posted to Holland to command the depleted German defences when he looked up and saw hundreds of allied troop-carrying aircraft and gliders heading to Arnhem. He turned to an aide and commented, "Oh, if ever I'd had such means at my disposal. Just once, to have as many planes as this!"

ABOVE: When the 82nd 'All American' Division was reformed in August 1942 it became the US Army's first airborne division. (US SIGNALS CORPS)

LEFT: British airborne forces were put through rigorous combat training before they were unleashed on the Germans. (IMPERIAL WAR MUSEUM)

Airborne Invasion

D-Day in Normandy, June 6, 1944

Allied airborne landings in Normandy had a key role in protecting the invasion beaches from German counter attacks during the vital hours that the landing force was establishing itself ashore. (NATIONAL MUSEUM OF USAF)

launching rapid counter attacks. The success or failure of the invasion would turn on the ability of the landing force getting ashore and setting up a defensible bridgehead. If German panzer divisions could drive the Allies back into the sea, then the war effort would be set back by years. With so much at stake, when the Allied supreme commander US Army General Dwight Eisenhower was told that the airborne force could lose up to 80% of their aircraft and more than half of the troops, he still ordered the air landings to go ahead. This was not the time for caution.

Three Allied airborne divisions were given the task of securing the flanks of the bridgehead. The US 82nd and 101st Airborne Divisions were to jump in to western Normandy to protect the US troops on Utah Beach from a counter attack by German 91st Infantry Division based in the southern end of the Cotentin Peninsula.

On the eastern flank, the British 6th Airborne Division was tasked to secure key bridges over the Caen Canal and River Orne, as well as the high ground overlooking them. Their job was to hold off the German 21st Panzer Division until the main British force was ashore on Sword, Juno, and Gold Beaches. Troops from the division were also to secure a heavily fortified German gun battery at Merville that overlooked the British landing on Sword Beach.

Further inland, the 4th Free French Battalion was to be dropped into the Brittany peninsula to help raise

O peration Overlord was the Allied plan to put troops ashore on the northern coast of France and drive German forces back to the Rhine. It was the biggest amphibious operation in military history with 132,000 troops being put ashore in Normandy from the landing fleet on the first day alone. To give the assault troops the best chance to get established ashore 24,000 Allied airborne troops were dropped inland to secure key bridges and terrain to prevent German armoured reserves

RIGHT: Pathfinder units were the first Allied troops to land in Normandy, marking drop zones for the main wave's airborne forces. (WAR OFFICE SECOND WORLD WAR OFFICIAL COLLECTION)

resistance bands to harass German reserves heading to the Normandy front. As part of the Allied deception campaign, hundreds of dummy paratroopers were dropped along the French coast between Le Havre and Isigny to try to fool the Germans into thinking air drops were taking place to the east of the River Seine.

At airfields across southern England on the evening June 5, US and British paratroopers started to board 1,200 aircraft and hundreds of gliders. Just before midnight the air armada took to the skies and headed south over the English Channel.

Pathfinders

The first wave was made up of small numbers of elite paratroopers, known as Pathfinders, who had the job of marking dropping zones for the main force. Once on the ground they set up lights and radar beacons to guide the second wave to the drop zones.

The stream of aircraft carrying the 6th Airborne Division had the easiest approach and they received little incoming anti-aircraft fire. The honour of the first British airborne unit to land in occupied France fell to the 2nd Battalion, The Oxfordshire and Buckinghamshire Light Infantry, or as they were more famously known - the 'Ox and Bucks', under the command of Major John Howard. His assault force was carried towards a strategic bridge over the Orne River in five Horsa gliders and it was hoped that their silent approach would give the attackers the element of surprise. Three of the gliders were put down with pinpoint accuracy right next to

the bridge. The Ox and Bucks were out of the gliders before the Germans knew what was happening. They took the bridge with minimal losses and soon Royal Engineers were dismantling the German demolition. It was a text book coup d'main operation that has entered the folklore of airborne forces. The Orne bridge was subsequently renamed Pegasus Bridge in honour of the British Airborne Forces who seized it.

To the southeast of the Ox and Bucks, the 5th Parachute Brigade was

tasked with capturing high ground around the town of Ranville. Strong winds dispersed the Pathfinders and the main force, but the paratroopers soon rallied their units. By 3.30am a follow up wave of gliders successfully landed six-pounder anti-tank guns to allow them to set up a blocking position to shield Howard's men from panzer attack.

Further to the north, the 3rd Parachute Brigade was landed behind the Merville battery and on five key road bridges in a marshy region

ABOVE: General Dwight Eisenhower visited US paratroopers before the start of Operation Overlord. The Allied supreme commander expected more than 50% casualties among the airborne troops but sent them into battle anyway because the fate of the invasion rested on their success. (US LIBRARY OF CONGRESS)

BELOW: Queen Elizabeth (The Queen Mother) talking to British paratroopers of the 22nd Independent Parachute Company, 6th Airborne Division, in May, 1944. (AIR MINISTRY SECOND WORLD WAR OFFICIAL COLLECTION)

behind the coast. Again, the landing force was dispersed by navigation problems and high winds. The paratroops were deposited in woods and swamps but soon gathered together and quickly secured four of the five bridges. Demolition charges were laid, and the approach routes closed down to prevent German counter attacks on Sword Beach. The final bridge in the town of Troarn was blown by a daring group of airborne engineers who raced through the German lines in a jeep. They dodged German fire to get to their objective before setting off demolition charges and then escaping on foot.

The brigade's most important mission was entrusted to the 9th Parachute Battalion, under the command of Lieutenant Colonel

although they missed their landing zones, the presence overhead was enough of a distraction for Otway to launch his attack. Bangalore torpedoes were detonated to breach the barbed wire entanglement and two assault groups raced through the hole in the wire. One group started to clear Germans from trenches with hand grenades and bayonets. The other group headed for the gun battery. When they saw the Germans had left the steel blast doors at the rear of the concrete gun emplacement open the paratroopers opened fire into the bunkers.

The surviving Germans quickly surrendered. Once inside, Otway's men discovered that the Germans had removed the big 150mm cannons that threatened the Allied fleet and had only left behind smaller 75mm guns.

The assault lasted only 15 minutes and allowed Otway to fire a flare into the night to signify to the fleet that the threat from Merville had been neutralised. He also released a carrier pigeon to fly back to England with the news. This was 15 minutes before schedule. The success came at cost. Nearly half of the 150 strong assault force had been killed or wounded.

Sword Beach Open

As dawn broke, British troops started to pour ashore on Sword Beach. They were protected by a ring of airborne troops. Although the 6th Airborne Division's drops had been scattered, its paratroopers had soon rallied and seized all their objectives. A German panzer counter attack against the airborne bridgehead was driven off by the 7th Parachute Battalion.

ABOVE: A Horsa glider takes to the skies to head to Normandy on June 6, carrying reinforcements and supplies. (AIR MINISTRY SECOND WORLD WAR OFFICIAL COLLECTION)

BELOW: C-47A Skytrain/Dakota aircraft of the 2nd Troop Carrier Group were part of the aerial armada delivering the D-Day airborne force. (USAAF)

Terence Otway. His battalion was badly dispersed in its drop and five of its gliders carrying vital anti-tanks guns never made it to France. Two hours after their drop, only some 150 men – a quarter of the battalion – had rallied to Colonel Otway. He had landed near a German battalion headquarters, and he had to fight his way to the rally point. With only one machine gun, a fraction of the required demolition charges, no Jeeps, no mortars and no anti-tank guns, Otway decided to attack anyway. It had been planned that the battalion would attack at 4.30am to coincide with a glider landing on top of the gun battery and Otway was determined not to be late.

On schedule, two gliders swooped down toward the battery and

RIGHT: Pegasus Bridge over the Caen canal was successfully captured by D Company, 2nd (Airborne) Battalion, Oxfordshire and Buckinghamshire Light Infantry in the first airborne action of D-Day. (WAR OFFICE SECOND WORLD WAR OFFICIAL COLLECTION)

BELOW: The Merville gun battery was a key objective of the British Airborne Forces. They had to knock out its guns that threatened the main landing on nearby Sword Beach. (RICHARD MATTHEWS)

At 1.30pm, Major Howard's men heard the distinctive sound of the bagpipes of Lord Lovat's 1st Special Service Brigade. The commando force had successfully linked up with 6th Airborne Division.

Out to the west, the US airborne divisions had a similar mission to their British comrades. Their job was to land behind Utah Beach and capture eight bridges over the Douve and Merderet rivers. The 101st Airborne landed in three parachute drop zones in the southeast of the airborne sector. To the north, the 82nd Airborne landed in three drop zones to the west of the town of Sainte-Mère-Église. Each division was then to be reinforced with heavy equipment landed in 52 Waco gliders just before dawn. A follow-up wave of 208 gliders loaded with reinforcements was scheduled for the evening of June 6.

The 101st Airborne Division led the way in 432 C-47s and it was scheduled to drop between 0.48am and 1.40am. When the wave of aircraft carrying the 'Screaming Eagles' approached the French coast the German coastal anti-aircraft fire open up a huge – if inaccurate - barrage at the incoming aircraft. The inexperienced pilots, many of whom were flying their first combat missions, took evasive action which broke up the drop formation and forced many of them off course. Fog banks made navigation even more difficult, and the paratroopers just had to jump when they were in the general area of their drop zones.

In the end, the 101st Airborne ended up being spread over an area 25 miles by 15 miles. None of the regiments or battalions landed on their designated drop zones in any strength. By dawn

the division commander, Major General Maxell Taylor estimated that he had only been able to gather up 1,100 of the 6,000 troops who dropped earlier in the morning. The remainder were spread around the battlefield in small groups. Many landed among German positions or in woods and swamps. The American paratroopers had been provided with 'clicker' devices that they could use to identify their comrades in the dark. During the confusion isolated Americans and Germans fought running battles among hedgerows or villages.

Major General Mathew Ridgeway's division fared better because its approach route avoided the German air defences. Its 369 C-47s kept their formation and the 82nd Airborne's Pathfinders had found and ➲

RIGHT: US Paratroopers of the 101st Airborne Division applied war paint prior to heading to Normandy. The idea was to look like fearsome Native American warriors. (US NATIONAL ARCHIVES)

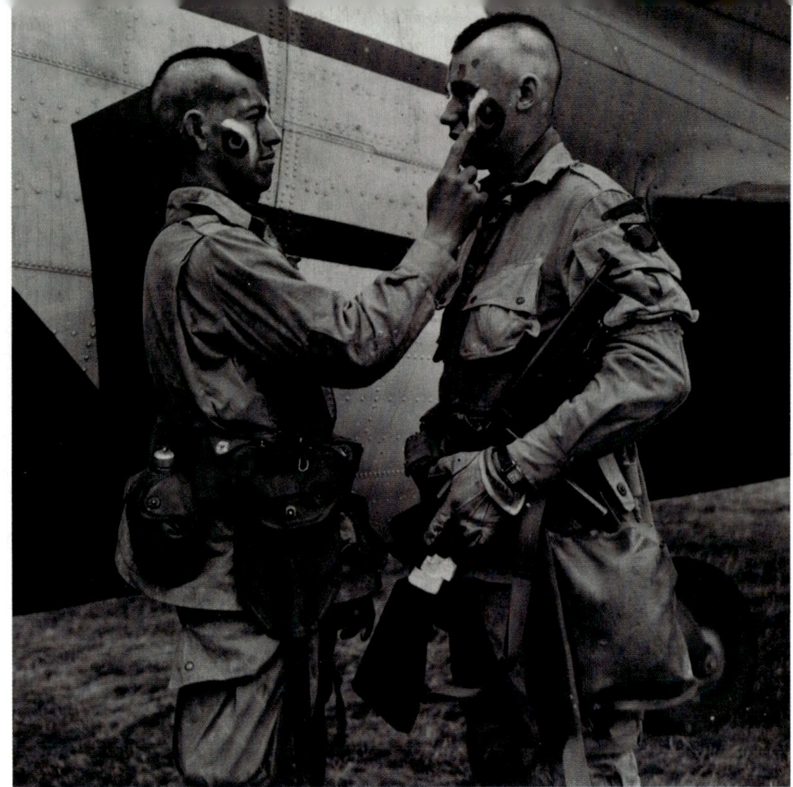

successfully marked their drop zones. One regiment, the 505th Parachute Infantry, landed half of its troops within a mile of its drop zone and 75% were within three miles.

The division's other two regiment's fared worse and less than 25% of their strength landed within a mile of their drop zones. Their remaining troops were spread across terrain criss-crossed with rivers and swamps making it very difficult to rally spread-out troops into larger units.

Paratroopers of the 505th Regiment linked up with local civilians who led them past German defences into the heart of the town of Sainte-Mère-Église at 4.30am. A German artillery battery tried to hold back the paratroopers, but they had soon driven the defenders from the town.

This lay astride a key north-south road and blocked the movement of

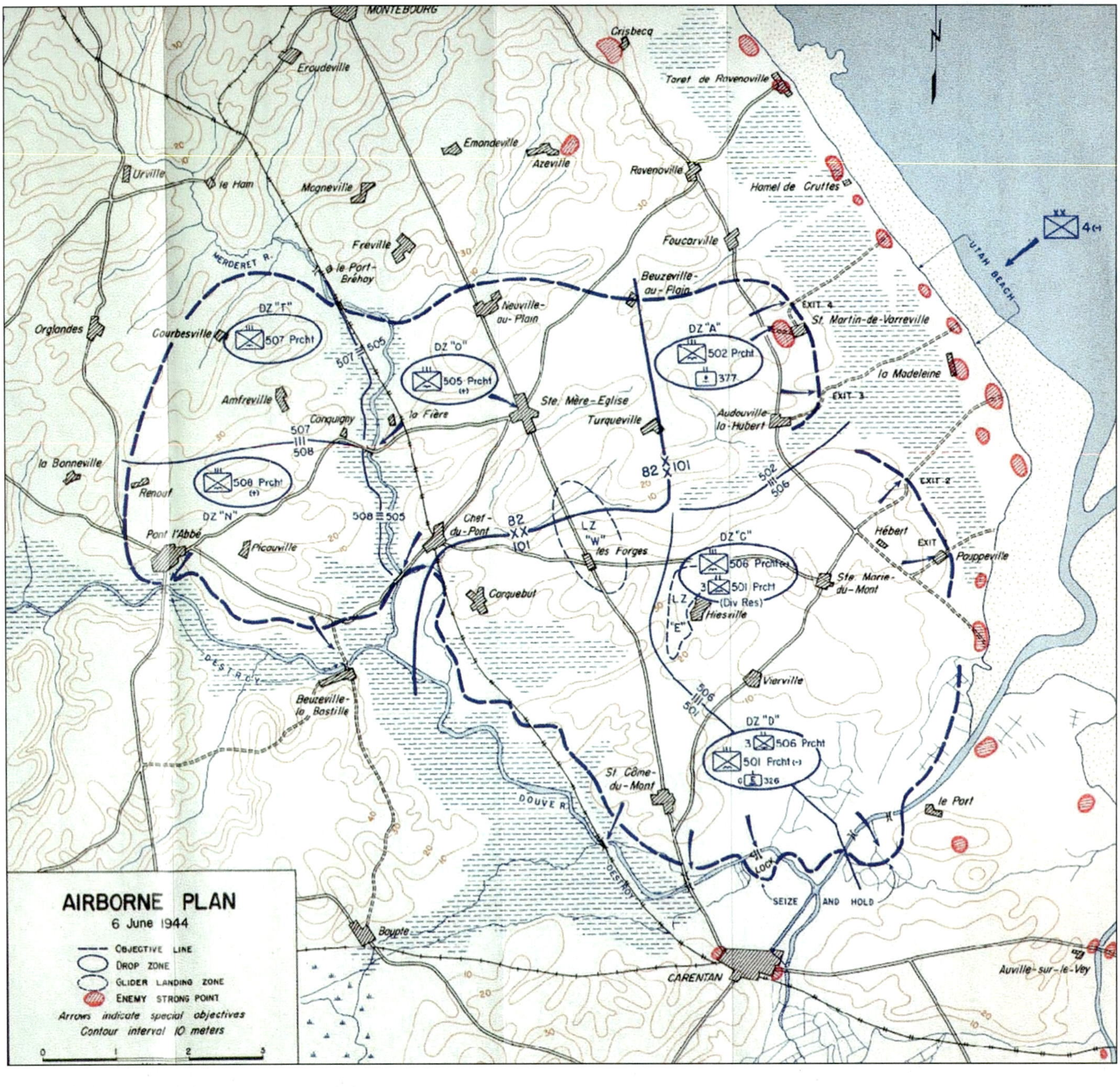

BELOW: The Normandy drop zones of the 82nd and 101st Airborne Divisions. (HISTORICAL DIVISION, DEPARTMENT OF THE US ARMY)

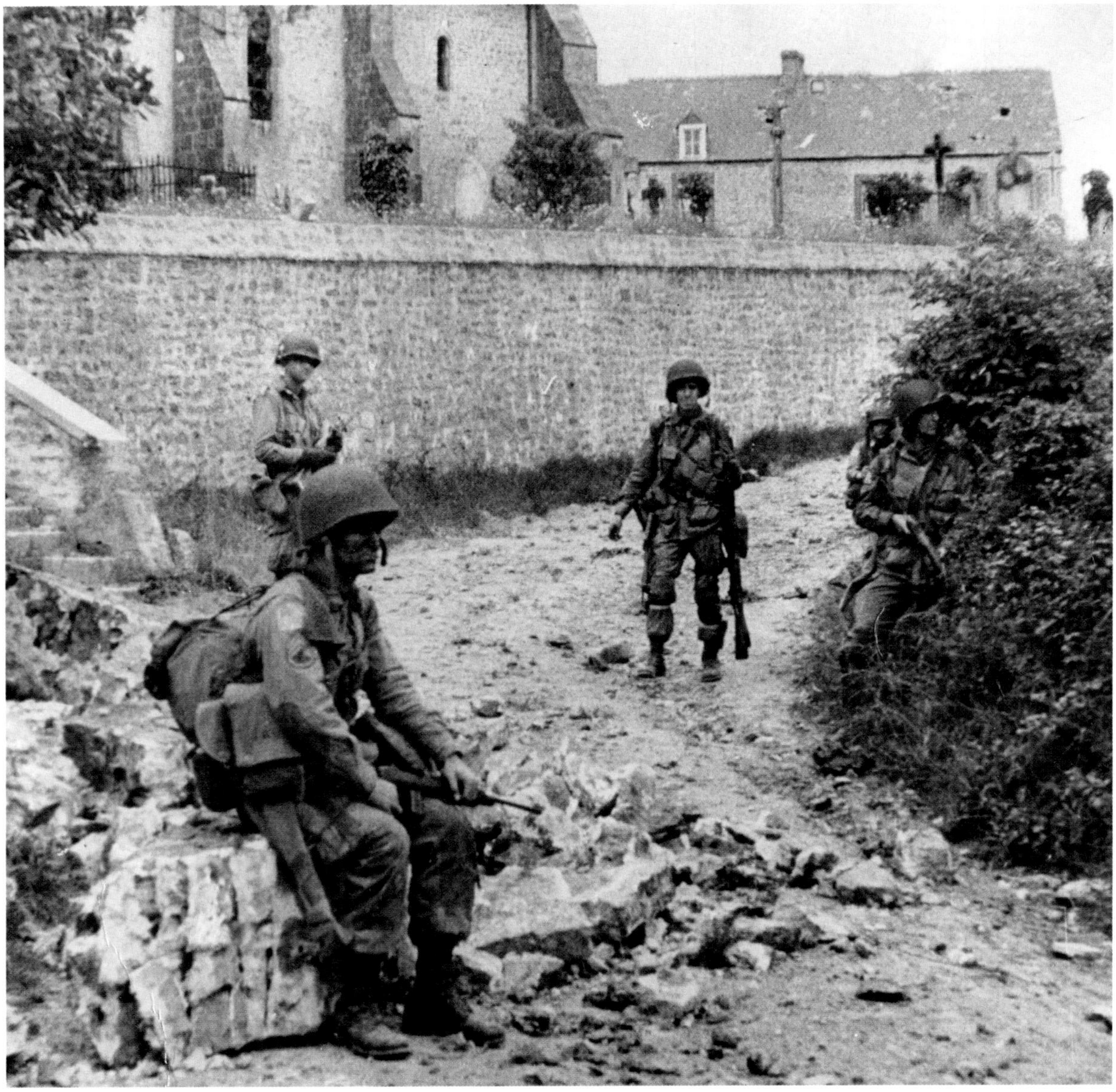

LEFT: A majority of US Paratroopers were landed far from their intended drop zones and had to fight in small groups among the villages and hedgerows of Normandy. Their exploits inspired the book and television series, *Band of Brothers*. (US NATIONAL ARCHIVES)

BELOW: French civilians rapidly rallied round to help their liberators, collecting supplies and identifying the German troop positions. (US ARMY SIGNAL CORPS)

German reinforcements. Smaller contingents of the 82nd Airborne attempted to capture bridges across the Merderet River but were rebuffed by German defenders.

Throughout June 6, tanks and troops of the US 4th Infantry Division pushed inland from Utah Beach and linked with the 82nd and 101st Divisions. Sherman tanks helped the 505th Regiment hold off a counter attack against Sainte-Mère-Église. On June 6 and 7, supplies and reinforcements continued to arrive by parachute and glider to help the cut off paratroopers keep fighting.

Carentan

It took more than a week for the 82nd and 101st Divisions to link up with all their troops and during this period they were locked in fighting with the German 6th Parachute Regiment, which arrived to hold the German line around the town of Carentan. In a tough fight the 101st Airborne took the town on June 12, but they were hit the next day by a large counter attack by Waffen SS panzer troops.

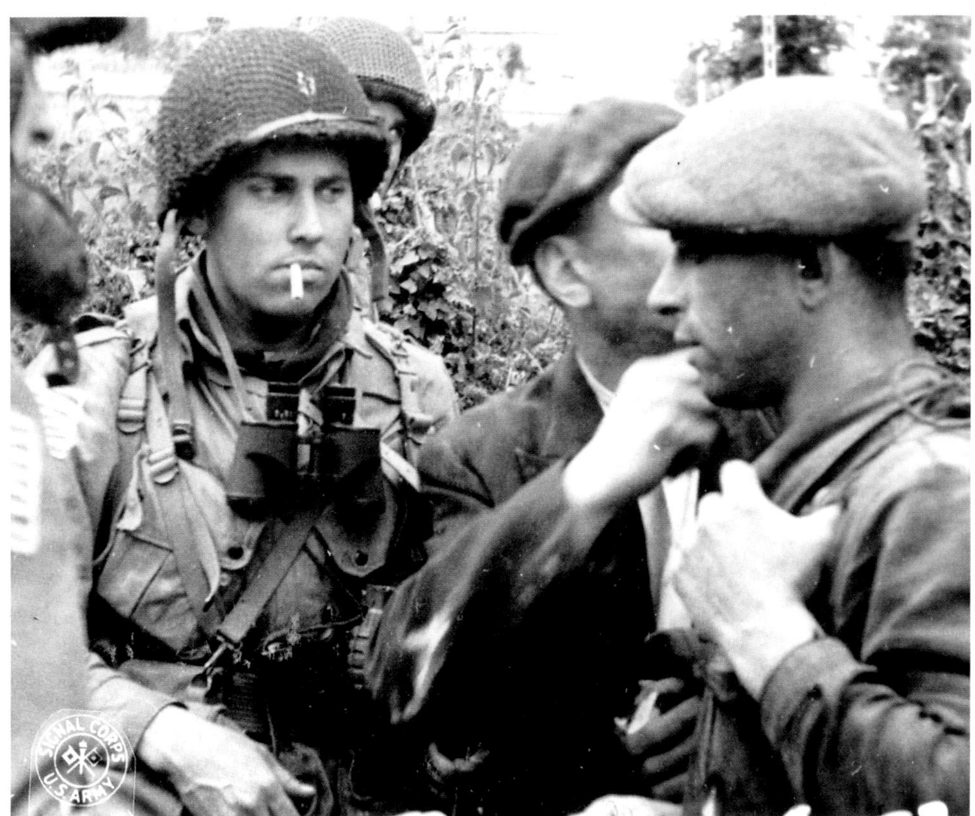

RIGHT: Mission accomplished. 'Screaming Eagles' of the 101st Airborne show off a captured Nazi flag. (US NATIONAL ARCHIVES)

US tanks were called up to drive off the German armour.

As more conventional units arrived on Utah Beach, it was possible for the Allied airborne units to be pulled out of the line to enable them to return to England to they could reformed as a strategic reserve force. The 101st Airborne was released from combat duty in the middle of June and the 82nd Airborne was back in England in early July. Their British comrades in the 6th Airborne were not so lucky and they remained in the line until August, holding the strategic 'Caen shoulder' on the eastern flank of the Normandy bridgehead.

At the end of the 'Longest Day', as D-Day became known, General

BELOW: Allied tank units soon linked up with the airborne forces to fully secure the Normandy bridgehead. (SGT. CHRISTIE, NO 5 ARMY FILM & PHOTOGRAPHIC UNIT)

Eisenhower's troops were firmly ashore on mainland Europe. Thanks to the airborne landings the Germans had been unable to launch a determined counter attack that threatened the Allied bridgehead. Although Allied airborne commanders were high critical of the dispersal of their troops across large swaths of the Normandy countryside, it subsequently emerged that this significantly contributed to confusion and chaos in the German high command. It was swamped by reports of paratrooper landings from south of Cherbourg all the way along the French coast to the east of La Havre. Hitler and his generals just could not work out where the main Allied force had landed.

This success came at a price. The 101st Airborne reported 1,240 casualties, including 182 killed, 557 wounded, and 501 missing. Its sister division, the 82nd Airborne, suffered 1,259 casualties, including 156 killed, 347 wounded, and 756 missing. The British 6th Airborne suffered around 800 casualties between June 5 and June 7, out of the 8,500 men it deployed. This was between 10-15% casualties among the airborne. The

USAAF and RAF lost 43 transport aircraft on D-Day, which was less than 4% of the committed force. General Eisenhower's fears about the losses to the airborne forces were not realised. The Allied airborne forces proved far more effective than expected.

The seizure of Pegasus Bridge, Merville Battery and Sainte-Mère-Église are now legendary battle honours for the British and American airborne forces. Generations of paratroopers that followed would look upon their D-Day forefathers with awe and respect.

ABOVE: Pegasus Bridge has been preserved for prosperity as a monument to the Allied airborne forces who spearheaded the liberation of France. (SIMCARD25)

A replica Horsa glider completes the Pegasus Bridge museum at Bénouville. (FODFISH)

A Bridge Too Far

Operation Market Garden, Holland, September 1944

ABOVE: Operation Market Garden was the biggest airborne battle of World War Two. (US NATIONAL ARCHIVES)

On the morning of September 17, 1944, the people of Holland were woken by the sound of thousands of Allied aircraft. Streams of transport aircraft and gliders could be seen heading into the heart of the country. This was the start of Operation Market Garden, the largest airborne mission in military history. The operation had the ambitious aim of capturing key bridges in Holland to open a corridor to allow Allied tanks to eventually cross the River Rhine and drive into the heart of Germany's Ruhr industrial region.

Since their defeat in Normandy in the summer of 1944, German troops had been in headlong retreat into Holland. The top British commander in Europe, Field Marshal Bernard Montgomery, was convinced that the Germans were on the run and one more decisive blow would finish them off. The normally cautious Monty came up with a dramatic plan to drop a 'carpet' of airborne troops into Holland to seize a string of bridges to open a route for his tanks to cross the Rhine at Arnhem. It was dubbed Operation Market Garden, with

RIGHT: The heroism of the Allied force and suffering of the Dutch civilians was immortalised in the 1977 war epic, *A Bridge Too Far*. The film was derived from the book of the same name by iconic World War Two historian Cornelius Ryan. (ROB MIEREMET/ANEFO)

Market referring to the air operation led by Lieutenant General Frederick 'Boy' Browning's 1st Airborne Corps and Garden representing the land offensive led by Lieutenant General Brian Horrock's XXX Corps.

At this point, Montgomery lobbied the Allied supreme commander, US Army General Dwight Eisenhower, to back Operation Market Garden over opposition from firebrand US tank commander, Lieutenant General George Patton, who wanted his 3rd Army to lead the Allied offensive further south in the Saarland region. When the German V-2 rockets started to be fired at London and Paris from launch sites in Holland, Eisenhower came under political pressure to neutralise the threat. At a stormy meeting on September 10, Montgomery persuaded Eisenhower

Arnhem. To try to leapfrog over the German defences, in a bid to seize a ferry crossing point and link up with Urquhart's beleaguered troops, the Polish airborne brigade was parachuted on to the south bank of the Rhine at Driel on September 21. However, the drop zone was raked by German fire and 590 Poles were killed or wounded as they drifted to earth in their parachutes. And, once on the ground the Poles found the Germans had sabotaged the ferry. The Polish troops then tried to set up a shuttle of inflatable boats to ferry supplies across to the British in Arnhem, but heavy German fire scuppered these heroic efforts.

By September 25 it was clear that Urquhart and his men could no longer hold on. Orders were issued for them to withdraw over the Rhine during the night using small boats and wounded paratroopers volunteered to man the front line to keep the Germans guessing about what was happening.

After the airborne troops had marched in silence to the crossing point, British and Canadian engineers started to shuttle them across the river. Eventually the Germans realised what was going on and opened fire on the crossing, bringing the evacuation to an end.

LEFT: The woods around Oosterbeek gave the British Airborne troops some protection from German fire. (IMPERIAL WAR MUSEUM)

BELOW: An increasing number of British wounded were collected in improvised field hospitals around the Oosterbeek cauldron. (SMITH, D M (SGT), ARMY FILM AND PHOTOGRAPHIC UNIT)

The situation was little better to the west of Arnhem where the remainder of 1st Airborne were trapped in a pocket close to their original drop zones. General Urquhart had narrowly escaped capture during to a visit to the front line and ended up hiding in the attic of Dutch family's home. He only escaped after shooting dead a German soldier with his pistol.

German attacks were relentlessly hammering the British lines and they had soon overrun many of the drop zones, preventing the paratroopers receiving supply drops from the RAF. The problem was made worse by the fact that radio communications had still not been re-established with England to organise alternative drop zones. Hundreds of wounded were huddled in an improvised field hospital in Oosterbeek in desperate conditions as medical supplies dwindled. Just over 3,500 British troops were still holding out in Arnhem.

The capture of Nijmegen bridge did not allow the British to drive north to Arnhem. Flooding had made the land either side of the single route impassable for tanks and the Germans had positioned heavily armoured Tiger tanks in blocking positions. XXX Corps was stopped less than 10km from

The operation successfully brought out 2,398 survivors. Unfortunately, 300 men had to be left on the north bank at first light. General Urquhart managed to safely cross the river but of the 10,600 troops of the 1st Airborne Division who had landed at Arnhem with him, 1,485 had been killed and 6,414 were taken prisoner. Around a third of the prisoners were wounded. Nearly 300 RAF aircrew were lost in the missions over Holland and the ground force was also hit hard, with XXX Corps alone losing 1,480 casualties and other supporting units suffering 3,874 casualties.

US airborne troops also suffered heavy losses, with the 82nd Airborne suffering 1,432 casualties, the 101st Airborne lost 2,118 and 424 US air crew were lost.

Much of Arnhem was flattened in the fighting and more than 500 Dutch civilians were killed, with thousands made homeless. The German defenders lost around

10,000 killed or wounded during the battle, a sign of the ferocity of the German resistance.

In the aftermath of the operation, controversy raged over whether the huge losses among the airborne forces were worthwhile and who was to blame for the failure to capture the vital crossing over the Rhine. Field Marshal Montgomery famously declared Operation Market Garden '90% successful' which prompted Bernhard, the Prince of the Netherlands, to ironically say, "My country can never again afford the luxury of another Montgomery success."

General Browning came out with his iconic comment that the plan was too ambitious, telling General Urquhart after he escaped Arnhem, "Well, as you know, I always felt we tried to go a bridge too far."

Heroism

Arguments continue to rage to this day on what went wrong and who was to blame. What is not in doubt is the heroism of the Allied airborne forces, particularly the surrounded British paratroopers.

The heroism of the British airborne forces resulted in the award of five Victoria Crosses, the country's highest

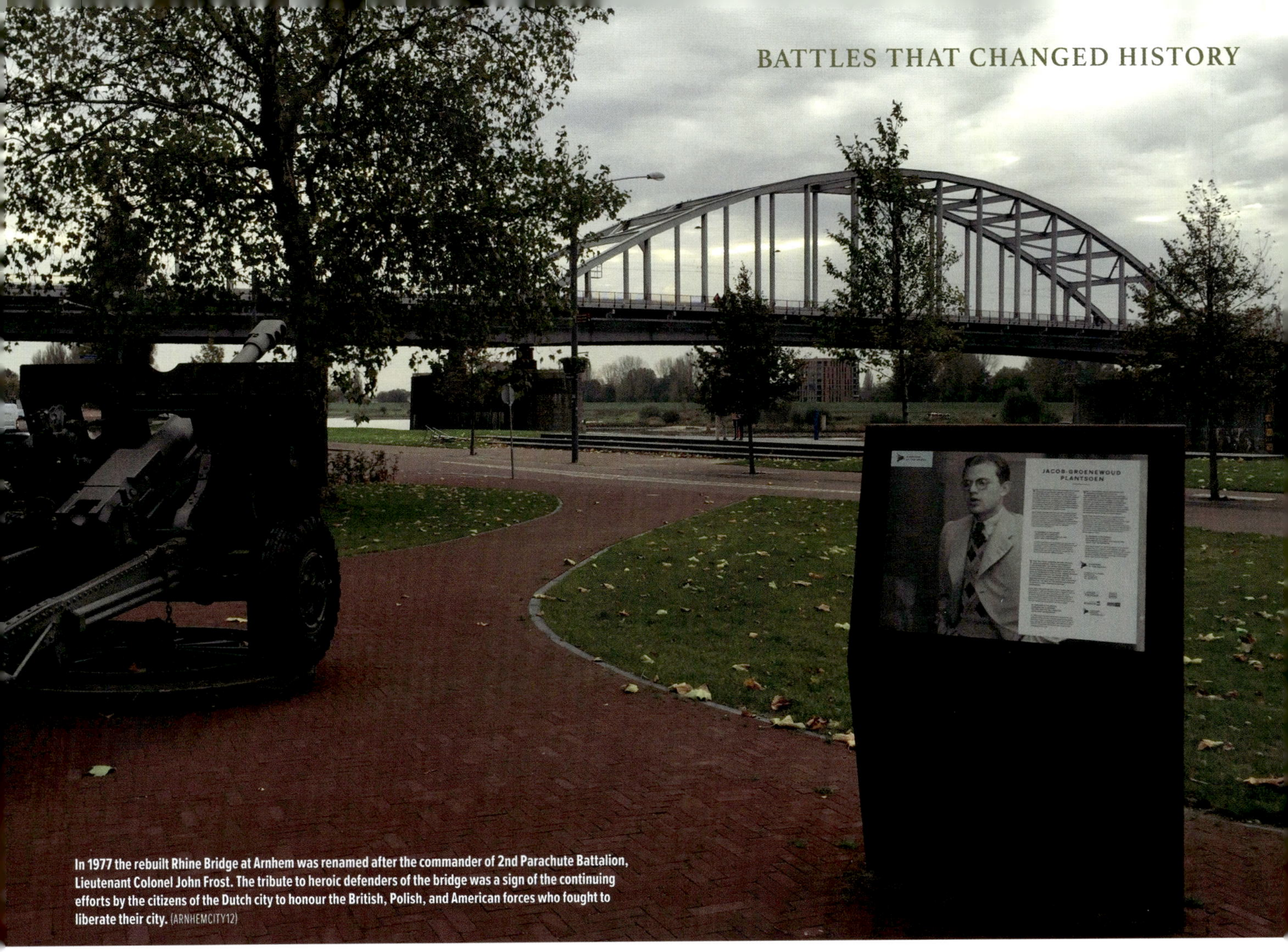

In 1977 the rebuilt Rhine Bridge at Arnhem was renamed after the commander of 2nd Parachute Battalion, Lieutenant Colonel John Frost. The tribute to heroic defenders of the bridge was a sign of the continuing efforts by the citizens of the Dutch city to honour the British, Polish, and American forces who fought to liberate their city. (ARNHEMCITY12)

General Urquhart's old headquarters at the Hartenstein Hotel is now a museum about the Battle of Arnhem. (AIRBORNE MUSEUM 'HARTENSTEIN')

award for gallantry. One went to an RAF Dakota pilot shot down on a supply run over Arnhem and the others were awarded to troops who fought in the rubble of the Dutch city. Two US paratroopers were awarded the Congressional Medal of Honor – the highest American award for gallantry in battle – for their bravery in Operation Market Garden. Montgomery spoke for many when he commented, "in years to come it will be a great thing for a man to be able to say: 'I fought at Arnhem'."

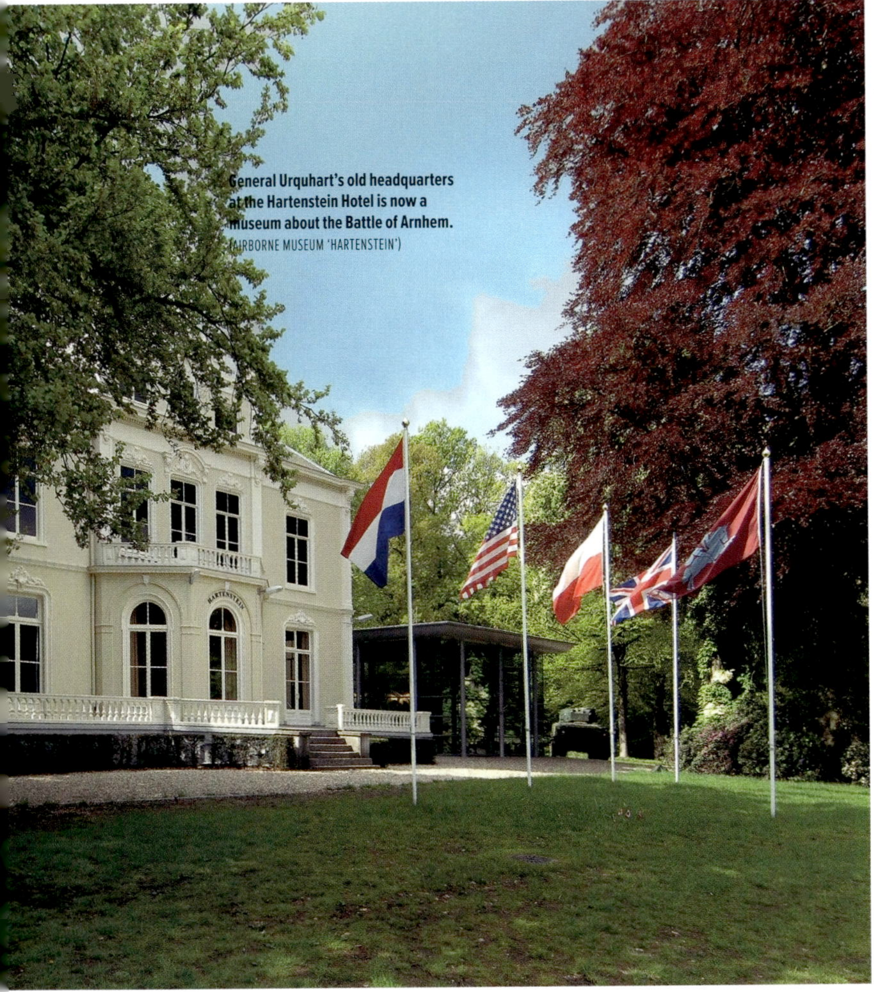

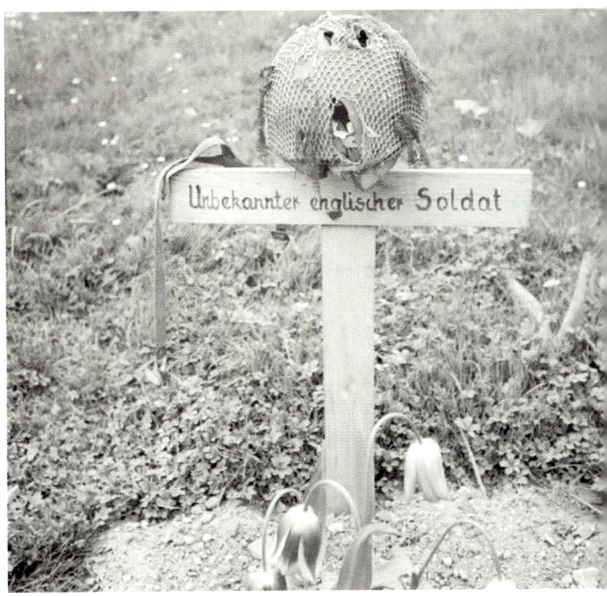

BELOW: Nearly 2,000 Allied personnel were killed in the fighting around Arnhem city. This included 1,174 men of the British 1st Airborne Division, 219 men of the Glider Pilot Regiment, 92 men of the Polish 1st Independent Parachute Brigade, 368 men of the RAF, 79 re-supply dispatchers of the RASC, 25 men of XXX Corps and 27 men of US IX Troop Carrier Command. (HEWITT (SGT), NO 5 ARMY FILM & PHOTOGRAPHIC UNIT)

Dien Bien Phu

ABOVE: French Paratroopers were surrounded and overrun in the Dien Bien Phu base in northeastern Vietnam. (US NATIONAL ARCHIVES)

RIGHT: Foreign Legion paratroopers, including many German veterans of World War Two, formed an important part of the French garrison at Dien Bien Phu. (US INFORMATION AGENCY)

RIGHT: French paratroopers landed at Dien Bien Phu in November 1953 to establish the combat base or hedgehog. (GAUTIER SAUTERET/CASSOWARY'S ARCHIVE)

France regained possession of its empire in Southeast Asia after the defeat of Japan in 1945 but the Paris government never managed to regain full control. The then French empire was known as Indochina and comprised what are now the modern countries of Cambodia, Laos, and Vietnam. A communist guerrilla army had been fighting the Japanese occupation since 1941, and it was not going to meekly submit to French rule again. Ho Chi Minh's army, dubbed the Viet Minh, retreated into the jungles, and began a violent insurgency against the returning French troops. Chinese communist forces supplied military aid to help the Viet Minh to launch attacks against areas held by the French. By 1953 the Viet Minh, led by the military commander General Nguyên Giáp, had grown to a force of 125,000 battle hardened regular troops and more than 300,000 militia units. In response, Paris had dispatched 190,000 regular French troops and recruited a local army of 55,000 troops.

The increasingly beleaguered French forces in the north of Vietnam were pinned down defending the main cities of Hanoi and Haiphong, as well as the coastal agricultural regions. French commanders were becoming increasingly worried that the Viet Minh would soon be strong enough to assault and overrun a major city, destroying French credibility, and threatening their control of Indochina. A series of major operations were mounted to try to destroy the main units of the Viet Minh, but they had always managed to escape back into the jungle interior.

This was the height of the Cold War. US and allied troops were locked in battle with Chinese communist troops in Korea, so Washington began supplying the French forces in Indochina with surplus military equipment, including fighter bombers, transport aircraft, artillery, and ammunition.

The French high command in Indo China decided to take the offensive against the Viet Minh by seizing an abandoned Japanese airfield at Dien Bien Phu, deep in the interior of the country. This would become a fortified 'hedgehog' base in the Viet Minh rear area and the French would launch raids from the location to deny the communists sanctuary. Further, the French Air Force would keep the garrison supplied by the air and neutralise any groups of Viet Minh troops massing to threaten the outpost. Nearly 12,000 of the best French troops were eventually committed to hold Dien Bien Phu.

French Spearhead

The French force was spearheaded by seven battalions of paratroopers who were battle hardened professionals. These included two battalions of Foreign Legion. These units are now the famous 1er and 2e Régiment étranger de parachutists, or 1er and 2e REP. The 1er Régiment de Chasseurs Parachutistes, or 1er RCP, one of the

oldest French airborne units were also sent to the base, along with three other parachute battalions that would later become iconic French parachute regiments. A battalion of locally recruited Vietnamese parachute troops were also dispatched into the jungle base.

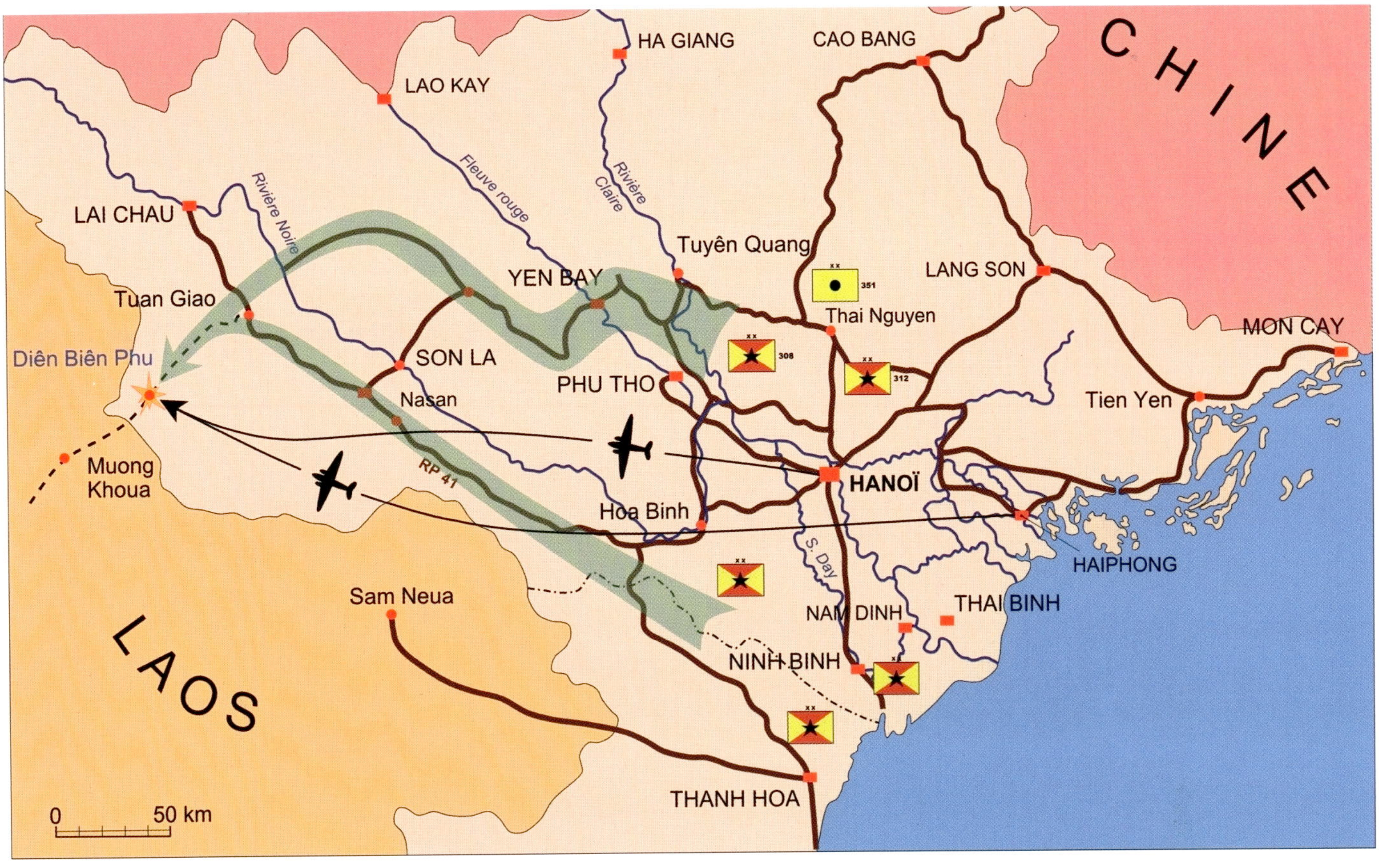

The operation to capture Dien Bien Phu got underway on November 20, 1953 with a jump by 1,800 French and locally recruited Vietnamese paratroopers. At two airfields near Hanoi 67 Douglas C-47 Dakotas were lined up and ready to go. Three senior French officers on board another C-47 had flown ahead and were soon circling over the area looking for signs of Viet Minh defenders. The officers detected no major concentration of enemy soldiers, and they found the valley shrouded in mist and drizzle. Just after 7am the mist cleared, and the officers signalled to the assault force that Operation Castor was to proceed as planned.

Soon the sky above Dien Bien Phu was filled with white parachutes and the French Paras were on the ground, forming up ready to sweep the valley for any Viet Minh. Unknown to the French, a battalion of Viet Minh regulars were based in the valley, and they were soon skirmishing with the attackers as they tried to collect their heavy weapons and supplies from parachute containers.

The French launched a major attack on the Viet Minh and soon the outnumbered communist troops fell back into the jungle. This brief battle resulted in 13 French dead and 40 wounded. Two more parachute battalions jumped into the valley the following day and they were put to work setting up a series of strong points on low hills overlooking the

ABOVE: The Dien Bien Phu garrison depended on air support to deliver vital supplies and to neutralise any threats to the base. (BRUNOLC)

LEFT: General Nguyen Giap masterminded the communist campaign that led to the French garrison being overwhelmed. (VIETNAM PEOPLE'S ARMY MUSEUM)

French troops returned to Indo China in 1945 after the Japanese occupation force surrendered but their grip on the colony was tenuous and communist insurgent forces were soon a major threat to the colonial garrison. (CLICHÉ ONLINE)

abandoned airstrip. Two bulldozers were dropped with the paratroopers to allow work to begin to clear the airstrip to allow C-47s to begin landing.

Over the next three months Dien Bien Phu was transformed into a fortified combat base, complete with a functioning airstrip, underground field hospitals, artillery batteries and miles of barbed wire entanglements. The air bridge to the base was augmented by a squadron

of new Fairchild C-119 Flying Boxcar airlifters, provided by the US as part of their aid package.

To protect the base, the French flew in 25 105mm howitzers, four 155mm heavy guns and 32 120mm mortars to provide long range firepower. They had 95,000 rounds of 105mm and 8,500 rounds of 155mm ammunition. Ten US-built M24 Chaffee light tanks were broken down into their components and were flown into

Dien Bien Phu, where they were re-assembled. Several F4 Corsair fighter bombers were flown in to provide close air support to augment heavy air support from strike aircraft based near Hanoi. The French were confident that their artillery and airpower would keep at bay anything the Viet Minh could throw at them.

Again, unknown to the French, General Giáp was already planning to build up his troops to overrun

LEFT: M24 Chaffee light tanks were dismantled and airlifted into Dien Bien Phu to provide armoured support to the garrison. (US ARMY)

the Dien Bien Phu garrison. The communist general quickly worked out that the key to winning the coming battle would be to neutralise the airstrip. If he could close it down with artillery fire, the French would not be able to bring in more reinforcements, or additional munitions. They would have to rely on air support flying at long range from Hanoi. With their life line cut, the French garrison would be slowly strangled.

Bombardment

Giáp ordered priority be given to moving up 144 75mm and 105mm howitzers, 48 120mm heavy mortars, 36 37mm anti-aircraft guns and 12 Soviet supplied multiple launch Katyusha rockets. Just as important was the building up of a huge stockpile of shells. An army of porters moved 150,000 through the jungle to the Viet Minh gun positions in hills overlooking Dien Bien Phu. These gun pits and ammunition dumps were heavily camouflaged to prevent French air reconnaissance picking up the troop build up. At the same time, Giáp massed 55,000 of his best troops, from the 308th, 312th, 316th, 304th and 352nd Viet Minh Divisions,

BELOW LEFT: Colonel Christian de Castries was nominally the French overall commander at Dien Bien Phu, but he suffered a nervous breakdown and command was assumed by a group of parachute officers. (FRENCH ARMY)

BELOW: In the early days of Dien Bien Phu, operation US supplied Sikorsky H-19 Chickasaw helicopters flew a shuttle into the garrison. After three H-19s were destroyed on the ground by Viet Minh 105mm artillery and one was shot down by anti-aircraft fire all helicopter flights to the besieged base were suspended in late March 1954. (NAVAL HISTORY AND HERITAGE COMMAND)

ABOVE: Dien Bien Phu valley from the air. The French strong points were overlooked by hills controlled by the Viet Minh. (TTXVN)

RIGHT: The handful of operational M24 tanks were repeatedly called upon to lead French counter attacks. (US ARMY)

RIGHT: Viet Minh troops picked off the French strong points one after another as the defenders ran out of ammunition and supplies. (VIETNAM PEOPLE'S ARMY MUSEUM)

battalion. Grenades were thrown into the French trenches. Hand to hand fighting followed as the Viet Minh cleared the French trenches and bunkers. By 9pm, the strongpoint had been overrun. Only 200 French troops managed to escape back to the main base, leaving 600 dead and prisoners behind. It had taken less than six hours for the Viet Minh to destroy a battalion of elite troops.

A new battalion of Vietnamese paratroopers was dropped into the garrison the following day as the French command contemplated a counter attack to regain Beatrice. However, bad weather grounded the French air force, so the attack was put off.

Giáp beat them to the draw. On the evening of March 14, the Viet Minh 308th Division was launched against the Gabrielle strongpoint. The single battalion of French officered Algerian colonial troops was outnumbered eight to one and had only eight 120mm mortars to provide heavy fire power. Overnight the Viet Minh troops swept through the strongpoint and by dawn only a small contingent of Algerians were holding out. The French launched a counterattack, led by six of their M24 tanks. They got to within 1,000 metres of the strongpoint and caused enough of a diversion to allow the 150 Algerians to make their escape.

The French garrison was now in a perilous position, with the airstrip closed and Viet Minh artillery raining down across the base. A senior French officer committed suicide and the garrison's commander, the aristocratic General Christian de Castries, retreated to his bunker. Effective command of the isolated French troops fell on the shoulders of the battalion

in anticipation of the final ground assault.

French commanders got a warning on March 12 that the Viet Minh would attack the following afternoon, but it was too late to do anything to forestall the battle.

The Viet Minh guns opened fire just before 5pm on March 13, targeting the two most northern strong points, codenamed Gabrielle and Beatrice, as well as the airstrip. Two C-47s and a fighter bomber were destroyed, effectively closing the base's lifeline. The remaining aircraft made a rapid escape to avoid sharing the fate of the others. The few French helicopters tried to continue flying into the base but four were lost to communist fire, closing down their operations.

A Viet Minh division surged forward towards the Beatrice strongpoint. Sappers blew holes in the wire, to allow the assault infantry to get close to the Foreign Legion

commanders. Morale was jittery as the French troops started to realise there was no escape. A battalion of locally recruited Thai troops slipped away into the jungle. Hundreds of other Vietnamese troops made the same decision and fled at the first opportunity. The closing of the airstrip was a bitter blow as it meant that any wounded could not be evacuated.

One-Sided Duel

At the end of March, the Viet Minh amassed two divisions to strike at the Dominique and Eliane strong points. This assault turned into a major artillery duel between the two sides, as the French tried to strike back at Giáp's guns. It was a one sided affair. The French held off the four day long Viet Minh assault, but they had to expend 13,000 rounds of irreplaceable 105mm ammunition.

On April 2, the 308th Viet Minh Division struck at the Huguette strongpoint but were also driven off by French artillery fire. A counterattack by Major Marcel Bigeard's 6th Colonial Parachute Battalion took back part of the Eliane strongpoint. This briefly raised French morale but as the number of wounded rose and the stockpile of medical supplies dwindled the situation looked bleak. By the beginning of May, the French were down to three days of full rations, 275 155mm artillery shells, 14,000 rounds of 105mm ammunition and 5,000 rounds of 120mm mortar ammunition.

At this stage Viet Minh anti aircraft artillery was inflicting heavy losses on the French Air Force, making it almost impossible for supply drops to reach the garrison. A large portion of these drops ended up in Viet Minh hands as the French enclave dwindled in size. Several attempts were made to drop reinforcements by parachute, but they always suffered heavy losses from Viet Minh artillery fire as they landed.

As more locally recruited troops deserted or retreated into deep bunkers, the French paratrooper units became the core of the defence. When a counterattack was needed, the Paras were called up.

Now Giáp massed his artillery, including his Katysuha rocket launchers, ready for an all out assault on the rump of the base. The attack began during the evening of May 1, and two of the last strongpoints fell ➲

ABOVE: With the airstrip closed the only way to reinforce the garrison was by parachute.
(WARNER PATHÉ NEWS)

LEFT: Several Viet Minh divisions were massed in secret in the hills above Dien Bien Phu in preparation for the communist offensive.
(VIETNAM PEOPLE'S ARMY MUSEUM)

RIGHT: CIA contract pilots of its front company Civil Air Transport flew air drop missions in support of French forces at Dien Bien Phu during the final days of the siege using former US Air Force Fairchild C-119s. Their US markings were hurriedly painted over with French Air Force roundels. Eventually 37 CAT pilots volunteered to fly supply missions from the French airbase at Haiphong. (JEFFREY W. BASS/ FAIRCHILD AIRCRAFT/CIA)

BELOW: French F4U-7 Corsair fighter bombers tied to neutralise the Communist artillery batteries hidden under the jungle canopy by using large quantities of napalm to burn away the cover.

within hours. The remaining French troops retreated to the heart of the base, where the hospital, command post and last supply dumps were situated. This tract of land was little more than a rectangle, a kilometre square.

A relief column was ordered to attack from Laos to try to break through to Dien Bien Phu and its spearheads got to within earshot of the battle before being blocked by Viet Minh defences. The French high command in Saigon was now resigned to the loss of the besieged base and proposed that the remaining 6,000 uninjured troops try to break out and head for safety in Laos. However, this would have meant leaving thousands of wounded men behind so French generals in Hanoi vetoed the idea as 'dishonourable'. The garrison was left to their fate.

The French garrison never formally surrendered to the thousands of Viet Minh troops who overran Dien Bien Phu's battered strong points. (VIETNAM PEOPLE'S ARMY MUSEUM)

Viet Minh troops marched the French prisoners off to jungle prison camps where they had to endure primitive conditions for four months while a peace treaty was negotiated between the French and Ho Chi Minh's communists. The deal was a humiliation for France, which had to hand the northern half of Vietnam over to the communists. It was the end of the French empire in Indochina. At the end of this the 3,290 surviving French prisoners were released. The remainder perished or were locally recruited Vietnamese who defected to the communist side.

The French defeat at Dien Bien Phu was attributed to over confidence and imperial arrogance. The French just did not believe the Viet Minh could defeat a large force of elite troops in a stand-up fight. General Giáp correctly worked out that the French force would be fatally compromised if its

supply line, via the air strip, was cut. For all the failings of the French high command, their parachute battalions went down fighting. The reputation of France's 'Paras' as elite troops was born in Dien Bien Phu and the units that fought in the battle went on to become the core of modern French airborne forces.

LEFT: Viet Minh commanders and soldiers proved more than a match for their French opponents and over the next 20 years would continue their 'war of national liberation' against the US-backed regime in South Vietnam. (VIETNAM PEOPLE'S ARMY MUSEUM)

BELOW: French prisoners were marched off to a series of jungle prison camps and they were only released several months later when the Paris government agreed to hand North Vietnam over to the communists. The defeat was a major humiliation for the French colonial project in Southeast Asia and within a year Paris had abandoned its Indo China empire. (AFP)

On the morning of May 7, Bigeard led his last two formed companies of paratroopers on a final counterattack, supported by the last operational French tank. The attack petered out and by the evening Viet Minh troops had overrun all the final French positions. There was no formal surrender. Individual French troops and officers came out of their bunkers under white flags and only 78 survivors managed to escape into the darkness and link up with the relief column from Laos.

The 56 day defence of Dien Bien Phu had cost the French 2,293 dead, 1,729 missing and 11,721 captured, of whom 4,436 were wounded. The French Air Force lost 67 aircraft and 167 were damaged in the battle. Giáp lost 8,000 killed in action and 15,000 wounded.

Operation Musketeer

Air Assault to Suez, 1956

As the tide of rebellion and unrest had swept their respective empires, the British and French sought to reorganise their armed forces to rapidly react to unexpected crises. Airborne forces offered the ability to move elite units to respond to sudden events with a minimum of delay. Both countries filled their airborne forces with professional soldiers so they could be highly trained and held at high readiness to deploy anywhere in the world. These rapid reaction units experimented with new tactics and equipment to ensure their global and tactical mobility.

During the 1950s the British grouped all their parachute units into a single entity, 16 Independent Parachute Brigade, which was then the only formation of the British Army trained to conduct large scale combat jumps. At the same time the Royal Navy had formed a standing

Colonial Influence

The British and French governments were furious at the threat to the international waterway and decided to launch an effort to overthrow Nasser and regain their influence in Egypt. The two colonial powers were locked in several bloody struggles against what was left of their empires and were determined to stamp down quickly on Nasser's defiance.

Nasser's move threw British Prime Minister Anthony Eden into a rage, and he immediately ordered an invasion force to be mobilised at British bases on Malta and Cyprus. Royal Marines of 3 Commando Brigade were massed on Malta as part of a large naval flotilla. The British Army's 16 Independent Parachute Brigade was sent to Cyprus along with a contingent of Royal Air Force Hastings and

LEFT: Egyptian leader Gamal Nasser was determined to end British and French control of the Suez Canal and relished the confrontation as way to mobilise nationalist spirit across his country. (MUSEUM OF AFRICAN ART (BELGRADE)

BELOW: British Prime Minister Anthony Eden was determined to deal the Egyptian leader Gamal Nasser a blow and nip in the bud any further challenges to British Imperial dominance across the Middle East. (HARRY S TRUMAN PRESIDENTIAL LIBRARY)

BOTTOM: Israeli paratroopers seized the Mitla Pass in the centre of Sinai Peninsula as part of the plot to provide the British and French with a pretext to invade Egypt. (AVRAHAM VERED/IDF SPOKESMAN UNIT)

force of Royal Marines that was ready to carry out amphibious operations around the British Empire. This formation, 3 Commando Brigade, was experimenting with new ways of projecting power ashore and the Fleet Air Arm had been ordered to establish troop transport helicopter squadrons to carry Royal Marines into battle from the decks of assault carriers. The US and French had experimented with using helicopters to move troops in Korea and Indochina, but the Royal Marines were the first military organisation to envisage using them in direct combat on a large scale. Today the tactic would be known as air assault or air manoeuvre but in the 1950s it had to yet to be christened.

France's airborne forces had been bloodied in Indochina. Even though several of their main parachute units had been wiped out during the Battle for Dien Bien Phu in May 1954, the French high command decided to

raise an elite force of professional parachute regiments to fight a growing insurgence in Algeria. These highly trained and motivated shock units would also be used to spearhead French interventions around Africa and the Middle East. France's aircraft industry built the revolutionary Nord Aviation Noratlas, which had rear opening clamshell doors to allow vehicles, or cargo, to be loaded directly into the rear cabin. A contingent of 36 paratroopers could be carried and dropped rapidly at low level through two doors on each side of the fuselage. The Noratlas first flew in 1949 and by the middle of the decade it was in widespread use with the French air force.

When the Egyptian leader Gamal Nasser announced in July 1956 that the British and French owned Suez canal was to be nationalised it lit the fuse that would lead to war just a few months later.

RIGHT: British and French airborne forces massed on airfields on Cyprus in the run up to the crisis. (DEFENCE PICTURE LIBRARY)

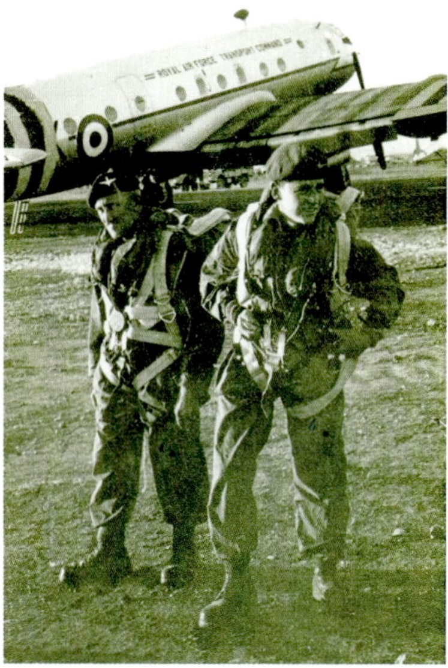

Valetta transport aircraft to drop its troops and equipment. The French dispatched their own parachute contingent to join the British Brigade on Cyprus and an amphibious force sailed from Algeria. To support the assault, strong air and naval forces were concentrated in the Eastern Mediterranean, including three British aircraft carriers and one French carrier.

To provide a legal and political pretext for the invasion, London and Paris hatched a secret plot with the Israelis, which would see the Jewish state launch an unprovoked attack on Egypt. In response, Britain and France would issue an ultimatum to both sides to 'withdraw' from the Suez Canal and allow their troops to arrive to 'protect it' from any accidental damage. The Israelis had already agreed to immediately abide by the ultimatum and give the British and French the excuse they needed to invade Egypt and retake the canal. In a secret meeting at Sèvres outside Paris on October 22-24, the attack plan was finalised. Within a week Egypt would be under attack.

The plot against Egypt got underway on October 29, with the launching of an Israeli offensive into the Sinai Peninsula. This began with a parachute drop onto the Mitla Pass to block the Egyptian lines of communications. London and Paris then issued their pre-planned ultimatum. Nasser refused to play along so on October 31 British and French aircraft began bombing Egyptian airfields in a bid to achieve air supremacy ahead of their invasion. An Egyptian frigate was sunk in the Red Sea, as the Anglo-French naval and amphibious force approached the Suez Canal. Carrier-borne aircraft joined the air offensive on November 1, and the bombardment continued for another four days until the combined British and French military command considered Egyptian defences suitably degraded. The invasion could begin on the morning of November 5.

More than 1,000 British and French paratroopers began loading and boarding their aircraft at Nicosia and Tymbou airfields on Cyprus just before dawn and then headed south. The plan was for the airborne troops to neutralise the Egyptian defences around the landing beaches for the main amphibious force.

First Drops

The 3rd Parachute Battalion Group and 16 Parachute Brigade's Tactical Headquarters began their jump on to Gamil Airfield to the west of the town of the same name. A few minutes later 500 men from the French 2e Regiment Parachutistes Coloniaux (2RPC) dropped near the waterworks to the south of Port Said city.

Escorting fighter bombers neutralised Egyptian anti aircraft guns and the troop transports

RIGHT: The French Nord Noratlas aircraft received its combat debut during the invasion of Suez. (PHILIPPE MATON)

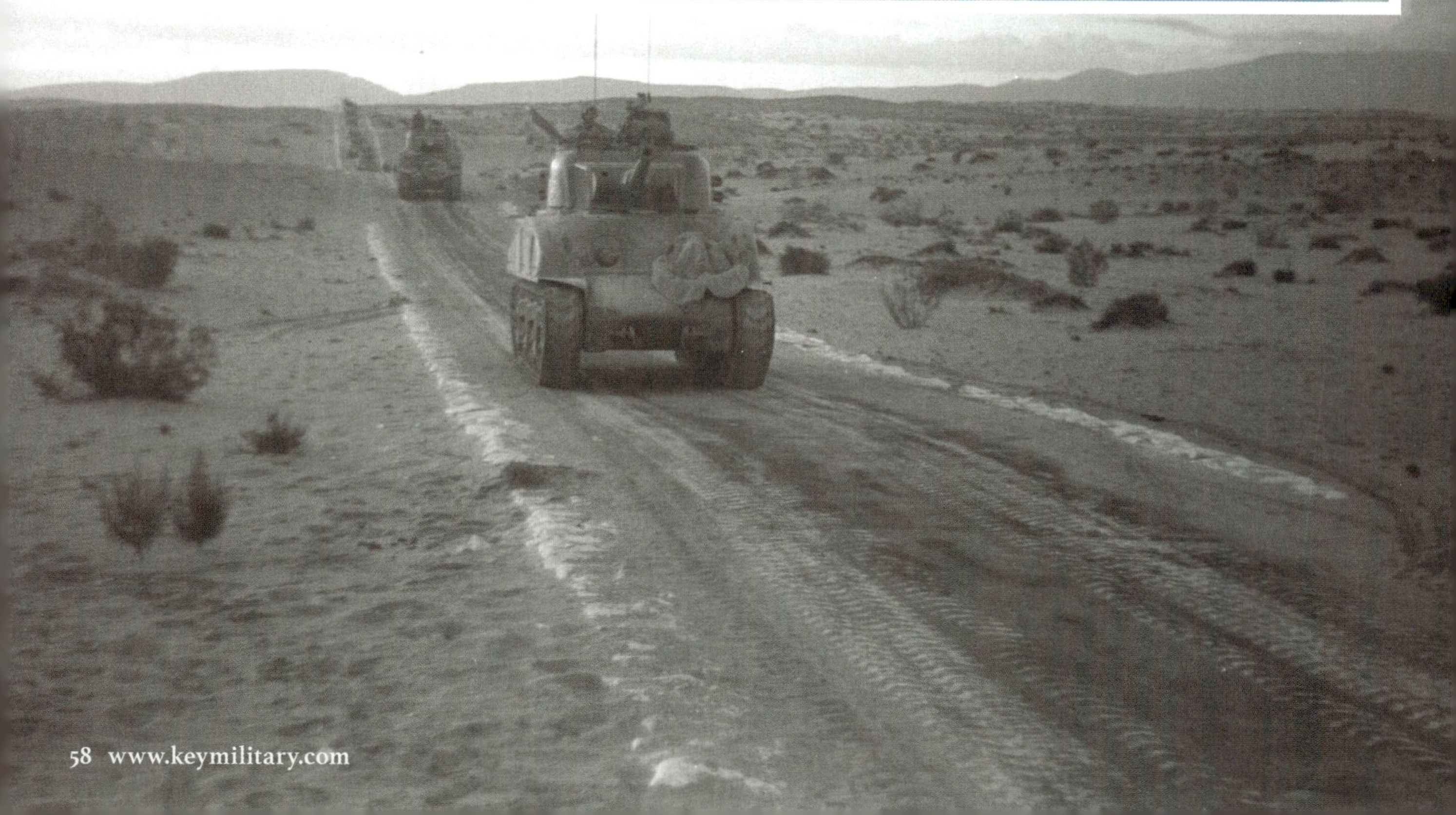

BELOW: Israeli tank columns headed across the Sinai on October 29, 1956 to set off the Suez crisis. (ISRAELI NATIONAL PHOTO ARCHIVE)

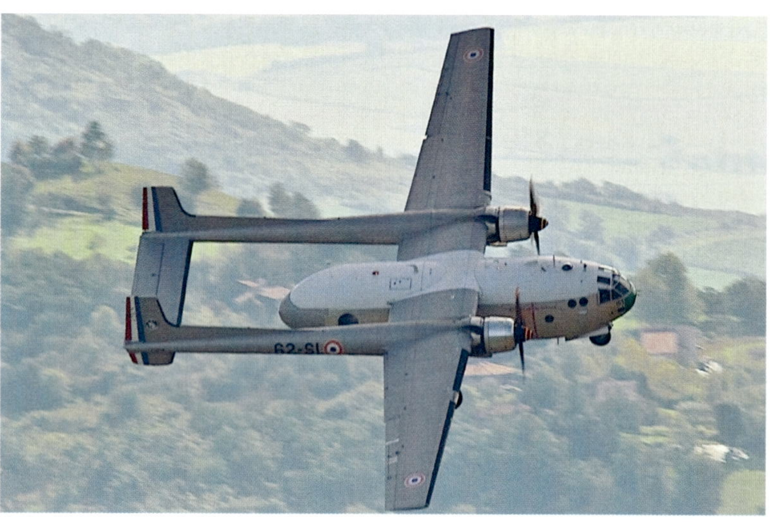

approached the drop zones. Nine aircraft sustained minor damage, but all of the first drop wave safely returned to base.

Egyptian troops and locally recruited militia put up strong resistance with machine guns, mortars, anti-aircraft guns and Soviet supplied SU 100 self-propelled anti-tank guns but the French quickly secured intact their two important objectives, the waterworks and the main road and rail bridge over the interior basin.

By 9am, the British paratroopers had cleared their objectives of defenders and shortly afterwards a Royal Navy helicopter was able to fly in to pick up several casualties. The battalion was then ordered to advance east towards the town of Port Said to link up with its French allies.

A rearguard of Egyptians in the Coastguard Barracks was neutralised by an accurate air strike by Fleet Air Arm Westland Wyverns and Hawker Sea Hawk strike aircraft called down by the paratroopers, but the British forces were still facing strong resistance. The Egyptian defenders used hit and run tactics against the British Paras and would bring up their SU 100s to fire at the attackers before quickly withdrawing. The lightly armed Paras had no weapons to take on the armour and had to call up naval strike aircraft to deal with them. A 'cab rank' of British and French aircraft ensured aircraft were always overhead, ready to be called down on targets by the troops on the ground.

A second drop of 100 reinforcements, as well as vehicles, heavy equipment and re-supply was made at Gamil airfield just after 1pm. Another drop by 2RPC was

ABOVE: British and French parachute drops around Port Said commenced on November 5. (DEFENCE PICTURE LIBRARY)

LEFT: As the fight for Gamil Airfield unfolded British helicopters arrived to evacuate the wounded out to the fleet. (DEFENCE PICTURE LIBRARY)

LEFT: Resupply drops started early on the morning of November 5 to keep the British Paratroops on Gamil Airfield fighting. (DEFENCE PICTURE LIBRARY)

RIGHT: The 1956 Suez Crisis. (DEPARTMENT OF HISTORY, US MILITARY ACADEMY)

made on the southern outskirts of Port Fuad, on the eastern bank of the Suez Canal. In fierce fighting more than 60 Egyptian defenders were killed before the French paratroopers secured their objective. Later in the afternoon the isolated Egyptian garrison offered to surrender but Nasser ordered them to fight on.

The British advance into Port Said was stalled on the outskirts of the city by Egyptian artillery and rocket fire. This meant the British paratroopers spent an uncomfortable night trading fire with the city's defenders.

In the early hours of November 6, 3 Commando Brigade started to put its troops ashore on landing beaches around Port Said. They brought with them 16 Centurion tanks of the Royal Tank Regiment to take on the Egyptian SU 100s. At the same time, a French landing force made up of Foreign Legion paratroopers of the 1e Regiment Etranger Parachutistes (1 REP) and Naval Commandos then landed at Port Faud to link up with 2 RCP.

As the British landing craft were approaching the shore, the Royal Marines of 45 Commando were on

BELOW: Whirlwind helicopters are loaded onto HMS *Theseus* in Malta before the Royal Navy task force sailed for Suez. (DEFENCE PICTURE LIBRARY)

the deck of the converted aircraft carrier, HMS *Ocean*, preparing to fly ashore in Westland Whirlwind and Bristol Sycamore helicopters. This would be the first combat air assault carried out by helicopter. The operation was carried out by 845 Naval Air Squadron, which had 10 Westland Whirlwind HAS.22s, and the combined British Army and RAF Joint Helicopter Unit, which flew six Whirlwind HAR.2s and six Bristol Sycamore HC.14s. These were first generation helicopters, with limited range and load carrying capacity. The Whirlwind was built under licence from the US company Sikorsky by the Yeovil based Westland. HMS *Ocean* and HMS *Theseus* were both World War Two era aircraft carriers that had been rapidly converted to operate helicopters in the run-up to the Suez operation.

Hot Landing

The commanding officer of 45 Commando led the way, taking off from HMS *Ocean* in a helicopter to over fly the landing zone his unit was due to capture in a few hours. However, in the smoke and haze the pilot lost his way and landed briefly in a football stadium held by Egyptian troops. They opened fire on the Royal Marines who rapidly re-embarked on the helicopter to make their escape. Despite the bullet holes, the helicopter was safely able to return to the *Ocean* so final orders could be issued for the air assault.

The commandos took off from HMS *Ocean* and HMS *Theseus* in 22 British helicopters and 90 minutes later, 400 Royal Marines and 23 tons of stores were ashore near the Casino Pier. They initially met no resistance but had proved that it was possible to move a large body of troops into battle by helicopter. As the battle developed, the Royal Navy helicopters then began shuttling supplies to shore and bringing back wounded for medical treatment. The British invasion force eventually suffered 96 wounded and the French had 33 wounded, the majority of which were flown by helicopter to a hospital ship.

For the rest of the day, 3 Commando Brigade and its supporting tanks started to clear the main areas of Port Said in a bid to link up with the British and French paratroopers in the east and south of the city. Many Egyptian troops discarded their uniforms and started to snipe at the British troops from roof tops and factory buildings. However, later in the afternoon a link up was eventually made with the 2 RCP at the waterworks.

Streets had to be cleared house by house and sometimes room by room. This took time and required a considerable expenditure of small arms ammunition and grenades by the Royal Marines. When stubborn pockets of resistance were encountered, strike aircraft from the Fleet Air Arm were called up to neutralise them.

International Reaction

The British and French intervention has met with furious international reaction. Most importantly, the United States government made its disapproval known by threatening financial sanctions against London and Paris. Later, on November 7, the United Nations called a ceasefire that was to come into effect in a few hours. The invasion force was ordered to stop its advance and an uneasy ceasefire settled over the battlefield. Thousands of Egyptian troops and armed civilians remained in pockets around Port Said and they continued to open occasional fire on British and French troops over the days to come.

Within a matter of days, the British and French had to agree to a humiliating withdrawal and the handing over of Port Said to a United Nations monitoring force which had arrived later in November. Then a full scale withdrawal was ordered, with the last of the British and French troops departing on December 22, 1956.

Operation Musketeer was a strategic disaster for the British and French. Their key ally, the United States had turned on them just as the operation was reaching its climax.

While the strategic objectives and execution of Musketeer were lacking, the central role played by airborne and air assault units offered many lessons. The initial parachute assaults had been professionally carried out and soon reached their objectives. Co-operation between the ground troops and carrier air support was effective and compensated for the lack of armour and heavy weapons among the airborne units.

The helicopter-borne air assault was a new development and the

subsequent use of helicopters to evacuate wounded rapidly from the battlefield would later become standard practice.

As the Cold War confrontation between the Soviet Union and NATO developed into a nuclear standoff, the role of large conventional armies boasting fleets of tanks and batteries of heavy artillery began to be questioned. However, the world in the late 1950s and 1960s remained an unstable and unpredictable place. The reputation of British and French airborne troops was further enhanced by the performance during the Suez campaign. They seemed just the type of troops needed to fight so-called 'bush fire wars' in Africa and Asia. When an allied government was threatened, civilians were at risk or insurgents were mobilising, then the call would go out to 'send the Paras'.

ABOVE: The first wave of British helicopters heads to Port Said. (ROYAL NAVY)

LEFT: Royal Marines move into Port Said to link up with the British and French airborne forces. (IMPERIAL WAR MUSEUM)

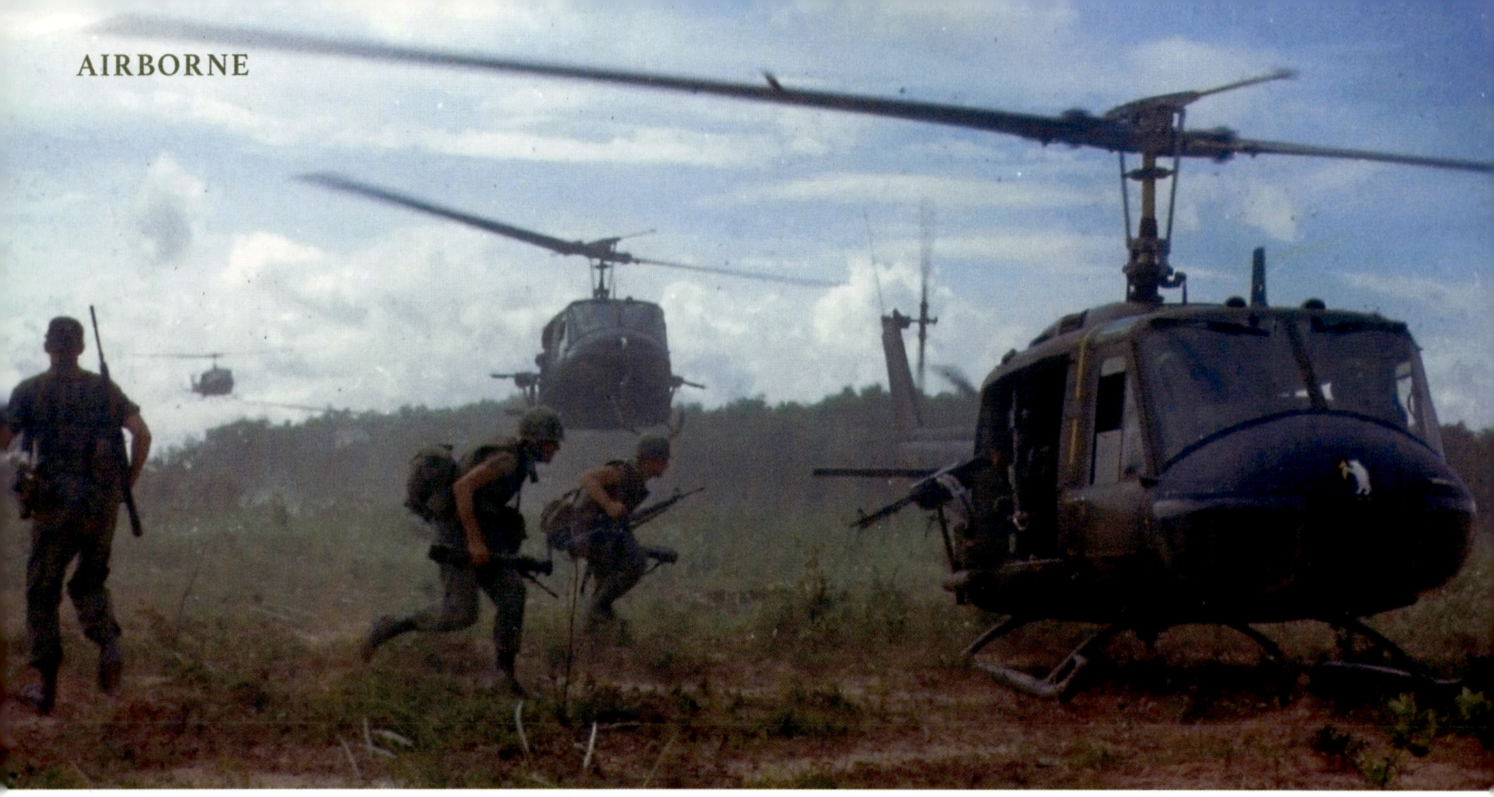

ABOVE: Airmobile tactics were pioneered by the US Army in Vietnam and the iconic UH-1 Huey was at the heart of all major US operations during the conflict. (US ARMY)

By Helicopter and Parachute

America's Airborne in Vietnam 1965 to 1972

America's long conflict in Vietnam saw the country's airborne forces in the thick of the action operating in what soon became known as the 'air mobile' role. The newly formed 1st Cavalry Division and the re-roled 101st Airborne Division became elite reserve units that were dispatched wherever the fighting was heaviest. They mastered the tactics and procedures of rapidly moving by helicopter and intervening in desperate combat situations.

Although the helicopter was the usual mode of transport for US airborne units in Vietnam, the 173rd Airborne Brigade also conducted the only combat parachute jump of the conflict.

US involvement in the Southeast Asia conflict steadily escalated during the first half of 1965 in a bid to roll back advances by communist forces. By the autumn of that year the US Army's only air mobile division would be in action in the central highlands of Vietnam.

RIGHT: The US Army hoped that by landing its air mobile troops deep inside enemy territory it would force the Viet Cong to mass to attack them, making the communist troops vulnerable to overwhelming American firepower. (LIEUTENANT W. H. BAKER, NAVAL WEAPONS LABORATORY)

At the end of June 1965, US President Lyndon Johnson approved plans to deploy the first divisional-sized US Army formation, the airmobile division, or as it was officially titled, the 11th Air Assault Division (Test). US Army chiefs felt the division needed a more prestigious title and, on July 1, 1965, it was officially retitled the 1st Cavalry Division and it inherited that famous unit's traditions and battle honours. All of its subordinate air mobile infantry and reconnaissance units adopted the titles of US Army cavalry units, including the 5th, 7th, 8th, 9th, and 12th Cavalry Regiments. The 7th Cavalry famously fought at the Battle of Little Big Horn under General George Custer. Its 1965 successor regiment adopted its Garry Owen march as its regimental song, while the 9th Cavalry adopted the iconic Cavalry Stetson. The move was a big boost for morale and the newly minted cavalrymen soon started to call themselves the 'Air Cav'.

Col Hal Moore

Within a few months, the 1st Battalion, 7th(1st/7th) Cavalry would win new

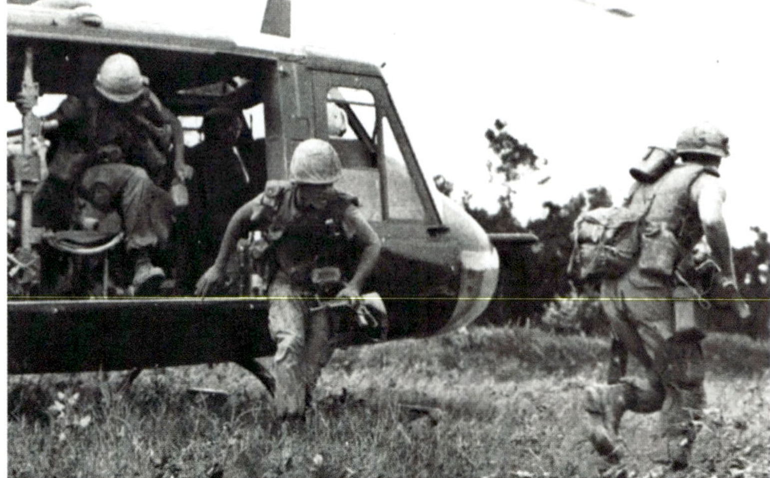

honours under their commanding officer, Lieutenant Colonel Hal Moore. He was a charismatic and dynamic, but thoughtful, officer who was portrayed on screen by Mel Gibson in the Hollywood movie of his Vietnam memoir, *We Were Soldiers*. The blond-haired Colonel Moore was jokingly nicknamed 'Yellow Hair' by his troops in a reference to Custer and he expressed fears that his men could share the fate of their famous predecessors if the US Army's new helicopter-based tactics did not prevail over the North Vietnamese.

The 11th Division was set up at Fort Benning in Georgia in February 1963, with the mandate to test and trial helicopters to fight on future battlefields. It was no secret that Vietnam was the likely venue for the division's first combat deployment.

Although the new division's organisation looked a lot like a conventional infantry division – it had three brigades, eight infantry battalions, an artillery regiment and support units – everything about it was orientated to air mobility. Helicopters were integrated into every unit and tactical procedure used by the division. The division had its own aviation group, with three battalions of air assault helicopters that in theory could move a whole brigade's worth of troops simultaneously in one lift. A contingent of Boeing Vertol CH-47 Chinook heavy lift helicopters were provided to move the fuel, ammunition, and other supplies to the division's forward operating bases.

Aerial firepower, in the shape of armed Bell UH-1 Huey helicopters, was integral to everything the division did. Gunships were incorporated into each of the air assault units to fly escort missions during air mobile troop insertion missions. The artillery regiment had its own battalion of rocket armed Hueys to provide fire support when the division was operating beyond the range of traditional tube artillery support. Armed Hueys and Bell OH-13 Sioux scout helicopters were grouped together in the division's reconnaissance battalion, or air cavalry regiment as it was known. They were the eyes and ears of the division and were tasked to fly over enemy territory to collect intelligence, identify landing zones, or LZs, for air assault operations by the air mobile infantry and strike rapidly at any targets that appeared.

RIGHT: Colonel Hal Moore led the 1st Battalion, 7th Cavalry into the La Drang Valley in November 1965. (US ARMY)

To pull Air Cav operations together the 1st Cavalry's commanders, at all levels down to battalion were provided with their own command Hueys fitted with additional radios so they could choreograph airborne operations as they unfolded.

Helicopter Force

When the 1st Cavalry shipped to Vietnam in the summer of 1965 it took with it more than 16,000 troops which was a similar number to the strength of a traditional infantry division, but it only fielded 1,600 vehicles - half those found in a conventional division. In the place of the legacy trucks and armoured personnel carriers, the 1st Cavalry took 400 helicopters. For the 1960s this was a phenomenal number of helicopters and even at the peak of US involvement in Vietnam in 1968, a standard US infantry division only boasted around 100.

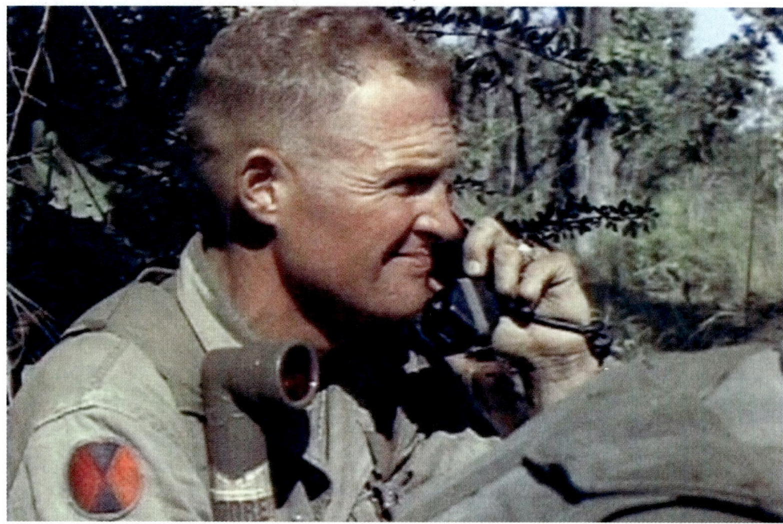

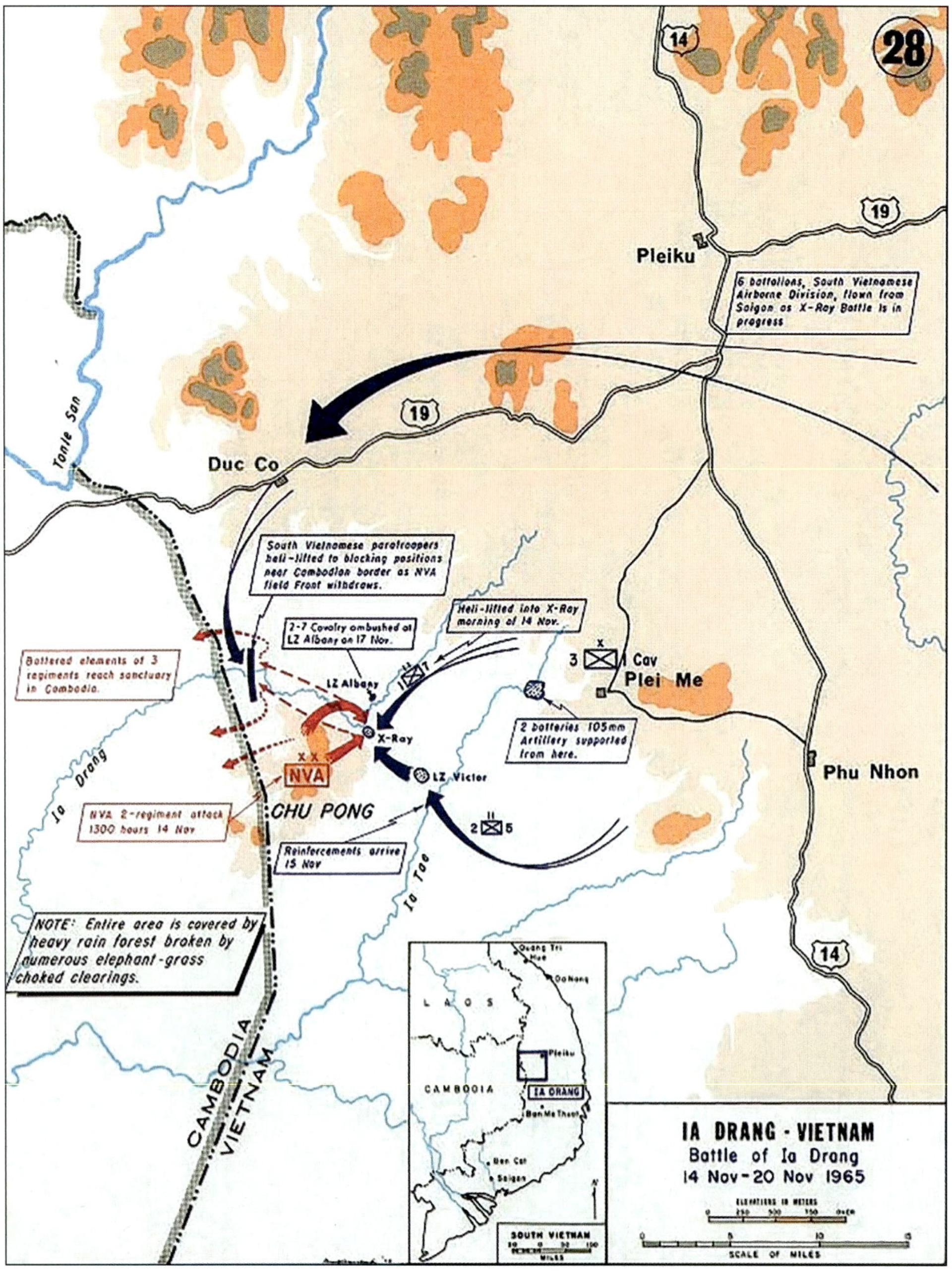

The 1st Cavalry was selected to lead the US Army's expanding campaign in Vietnam because the Pentagon thought the division's mobility and firepower would give it an edge over the Viet Cong and their North Vietnamese allies. The communist force up to 1965 had relied on light infantry tactics to infiltrate government-controlled regions and

BELOW: The Battle of the La Drang Valley. (US ARMY)

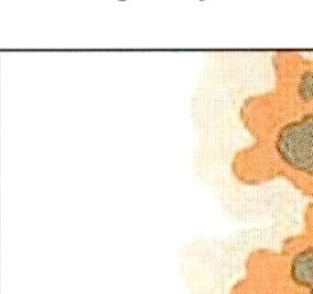

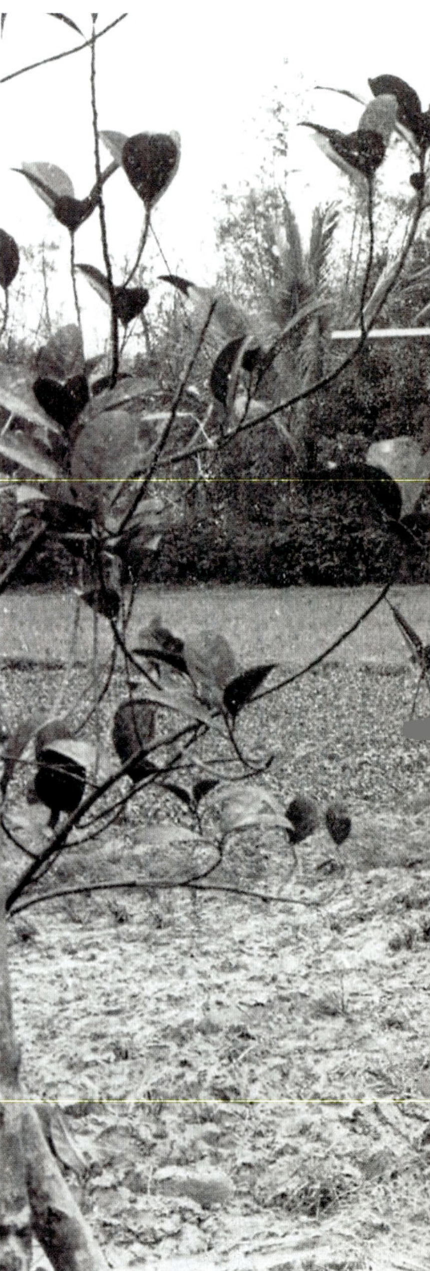

launch surprise attacks to overwhelm isolated detachments of the Army of the Republic of Vietnam or ARVN. It was hoped that the helicopters of the 1st Cavalry would allow the US Army to turn the tables on the Viet Cong by rapidly inserting US troops inside their territory to either capture key headquarters and supply dumps or force the communists to mass their troops to counterattack. Once the communists had joined battle, their troops would become vulnerable to overwhelming US firepower. That at least was the theory. It would be put to the test for real for the first time in October and November 1965 when the 1st Cavalry was dispatched to Pleiku Province in the central highlands to counter a suspected build up of North Vietnamese troops.

On November 13, Colonel Moore and his 1st/7th Cavalry were ordered to launch the 1st Cavalry's first ever battalion-sized air assault operations into the la Drang Valley area, where a large concentration of North Vietnamese troops were believed to be based.

After first light on the following morning, four scout Hueys of the 1st/9th Cavalry flew a low level 'map-of-the-earth' reconnaissance mission over the target areas to try to find signs of the enemy and confirm the status of the proposed landing zones. After a 40-minute flight, the

LEFT: Mighty CH-47 Chinooks moved all of the 1st Cavalry Division's supplies and ammunition to forward operating bases to keep its troops and UH-1s in the fight. (ICEMANWCS)

BELOW: The 101st Airborne Division was the second divisional-sized air mobile formation in Vietnam. (US ARMY)

ABOVE: US firepower including USAF B-52 'Arc Light' carpet bombing strikes increased during the final years of the American presence in Vietnam in a bid to reduce US casualties. (USAF)

the fringe of the landing zone ready to open fire as the first helicopters disgorged their troops.

The calm would not last long. Elements of three North Vietnamese regiments were nearby and they were immediately ordered to strike at the Americans who had just landed in their midst.

The next two days saw the 1st/7th Cavalry fight for its life as the communist troops attempted to overwhelm their positions. LZ X-Ray was a flat clearing with scrub trees, anthills and thick elephant grass stretching out to the edge of the jungle. Colonel Moore set up his tactical headquarters in the centre of the clearing next to a small resupply landing zone that could take two Hueys at a time. His troops fanned out to form a perimeter and they started to probe into the jungle.

By afternoon, the first contacts were reported around the perimeter and soon waves of North Vietnamese were attacking the US troops. One platoon was cut off and the rest of the Cavalrymen went firm in their positions and tried to repel the human wave of communist troops.

The 1st/7th Cavalry's command team called up air and artillery fire.

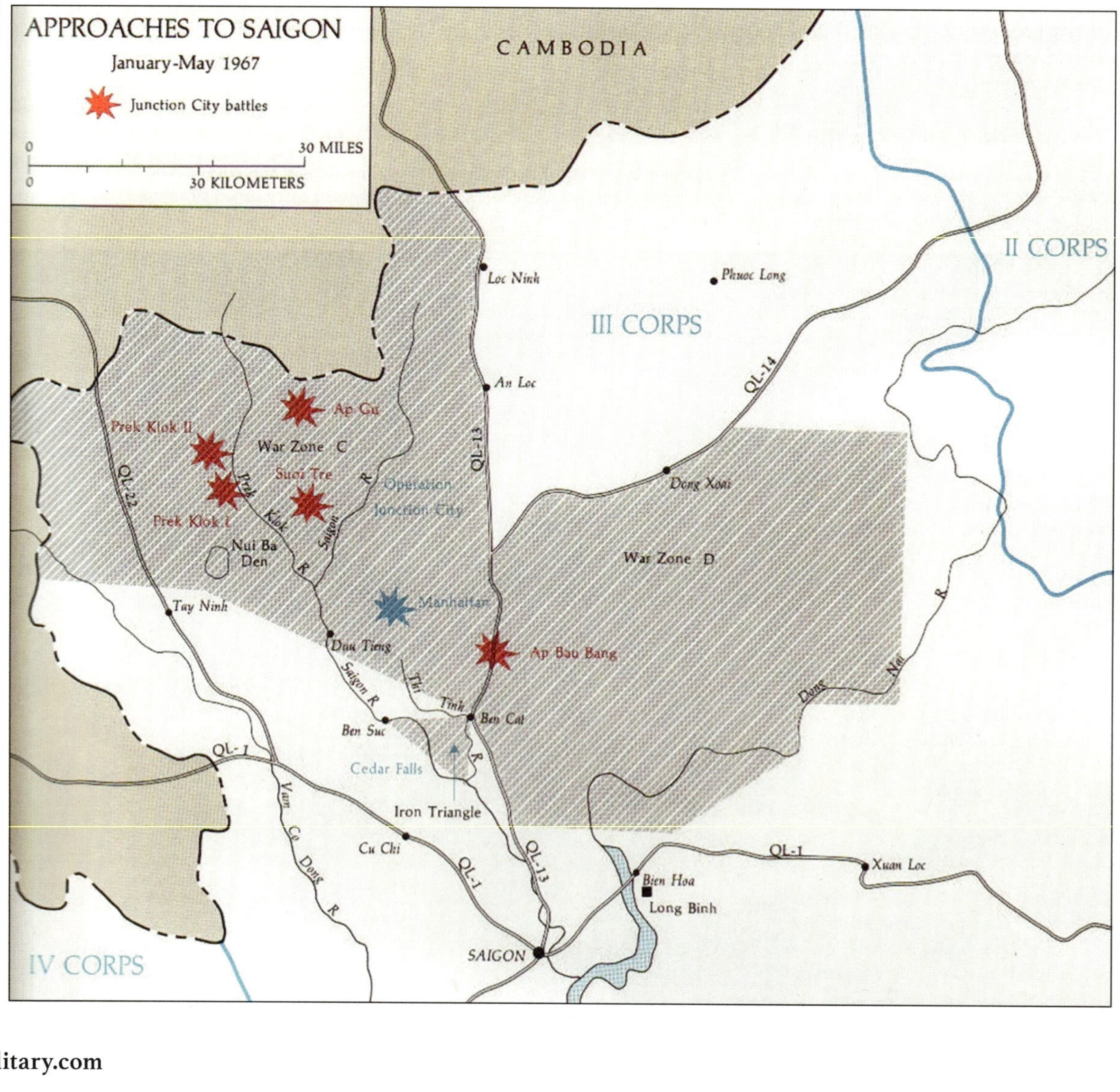

scouts returned to Colonel Moore's forward operating base at Plei Me. They did not take any fire or spot any enemy troops. More importantly, they reported that one of the landing zones, code name LZ X-Ray looked the most suitable because it

could take up to 10 Hueys at time, maximising the number of soldiers Colonel Moore could move in each wave of helicopters or lift.

The air assault phase of the operation proved anti-climatic. There were no communist troops dug-in around

APPROACHES TO SAIGON

RIGHT: Operation Junction City. (US ARMY CENTER OF MILITARY HISTORY)

ammunition heading into LZ X-Ray, as well as bringing out wounded Cavalrymen.

Senior US commanders were full of praise of Colonel Moore and his cavalrymen. The top US commander in Vietnam, General William Westmoreland, stated: "the ability of the Americans to meet and defeat the best troops the enemy could put on the field of battle was once more demonstrated beyond any doubt, as was the validity of the US Army's airmobile concept."

General Westmoreland and the Pentagon immediately requested that more helicopters and air mobile

LEFT: Columns of M113 armoured personnel carriers swept into action to drive Viet Cong fighters onto the cordon set up by the 173rd Airborne Brigade during Operation Junction City. (US ARMY)

BELOW: A flank security position anchored by men of the 173 Airborne Brigade during the conduct of Operation Junction City. (US ARMY)

Soon USAF fast jets were rolling in to bomb enemy troop concentrations and artillery fire was raining down. Completing the fire support were Huey gunships who blasted enemy positions with rockets and machine guns. This continued throughout the afternoon as wave after wave of attackers surged towards the tight US perimeter.

Night prevented the air support continuing and during the darkness, Colonel Moore and his men had to rely on artillery fire for protection. At dawn, the battle resumed again with more human wave attacks coming in a bid to overrun the US lines. Again, Colonel Moore and his command team choreographed strike jets and Huey gunships to keep the enemy at bay.

Just before 8am the battle reached its climax. In a bid to make it impossible for the US to use its airpower and artillery, the communists surged forward to within grenade throwing range of the Cavalry lines. US commanders popped smoke on their positions so the gunship pilots could identify the friendly lines and allow them to put down rockets within a few dozen metres of the Cavalrymen. This barrage broke the back of the communist attack. Later in the morning the communists pulled back, leaving hundreds of dead behind. Colonel Moore estimated that 634 North Vietnamese soldiers had died in the battle.

No Little Big Horn

Colonel Moore and his men did not share the fate of their predecessors at the Little Big Horn. Gunship, fast jet, and artillery support kept the communist troops at bay and the Huey pilots kept a nonstop flow of

ABOVE: Wounded 101st Airborne soldiers being loaded onto a UH-1 medevac helicopter during the Battle for Hamburger Hill. (UNITED STATES ARMY MILITARY HISTORY INSTITUTE)

BELOW: A soldier observes a supply airdrop conducted by a C-130 Hercules airlifter during Operation Junction City. (US ARMY)

units be sent to Vietnam. Over the next seven years the number and size of helicopter equipped US Army units surged. At the peak of the conflict there were two air assault divisions, the 1st Cavalry Division and 101st Airborne Division (Airmobile), in Vietnam. Each had more than 400 helicopters to allow them to manoeuvre across the battlefield by air. Other US Army divisions had their own air assault battalion to allow them to conduct local air mobility operations around their own area of responsibility.

The US Army's airborne units arrived in South Vietnam in a piecemeal fashion. First to arrive in

May 1965 was the Okinawa based 173rd Airborne Brigade, which was the Pacific region reserve force. Then in July 1966, the 1st Brigade of the 101st Airborne Division landed in the country. These two brigades operated as rapid reaction units, moving from region to region where locally based troops needed bolstering with elite infantry forces. They got plenty of exercise flying into action in Hueys and Chinooks but did not have their own dedicated helicopters attached to them at this stage.

As the war escalated General Westmoreland launched bigger and bigger search and destroy missions in a bid to flush out Vietcong insurgents and North Vietnamese regulars hiding in South Vietnam's jungles. The enemy proved increasingly reluctant to stand and fight against superior US firepower. Air mobile units offered a way to fly US troops deep into the jungle to set up cordons to trap communists from escaping search and destroy sweeps. Eventually, the communist commanders started to learn how to predict helicopter assaults. So, in February 1967, Westmoreland came up with a new plan.

A battalion of the 173rd Brigade would be parachuted into a landing zone close to the Cambodian border to set up a blocking position as seven US and four ARVN battalions tried to flush out a division of North Vietnamese. More than 250 US helicopters flew other US units to set up more blocking positions. This was the first US combat parachute drop since the Korean War 15 years earlier.

Junction City

Operation Junction City kicked off on February 22 with the jump from 16 Lockheed C-130 Hercules by the 2nd Battalion, 503rd Infantry Regiment into an open paddy field in Tay Ninh province. The jump caught the enemy by surprise and the 845 descending paratroopers only came under ineffective fire, with just 11 soldiers suffering minor jump injuries. The brigade commander, Brigadier General John R. Deane, jumped in the first wave.

The Americans quickly rallied and set up a defensive perimeter

and waited for a second wave of aircraft carrying a battery of 105mm howitzers, mortars and other equipment. Soon afterwards more C-130s started to deliver artillery ammunition and supplies to the paratroopers using the new Cargo Delivery Systems, which pulled pallets out the aircraft rear ramp as it made a low level pass over a drop zone. With its fire base set up, the paratroopers started to send out patrols to dominate the North Vietnamese escape routes. As the battle developed, the enemy made their escape in small groups.

By the time Operation Junction City was concluded in May 1967, the US military claimed 2,728 enemy killed and 34 prisoners taken, along with 100 crew-served weapons, 491 individual weapons, and thousands of rounds of ammunition, grenades, and mines.

The 101st Airborne's 1st Brigade was also alerted to join Operation Junction City, but its jump was not needed. Although the 173rd Brigade's jump was judged a tactical success, this was the only battalion or company level combat jump of the Vietnam conflict.

In December 1967, the remainder of the 101st Airborne Division had deployed to South Vietnam, and it was soon engaged in heavy combat during the 1968 Tet Offensive, operating mainly in the north of the country. Alongside US Marine Corps units, the 101st Airborne was set to recapture the city of Hue from the communists. In perhaps its most high profile operation of the hostilities, a platoon from C Company, 1st Battalion, 502nd Infantry was airlifted by helicopter on to the roof of the US Embassy ❯

ABOVE: Air strikes and artillery fire during the Battle of Hamburger Hill turned the battlefield into a moonscape.
(UNITED STATES ARMY MILITARY HISTORY INSTITUTE)

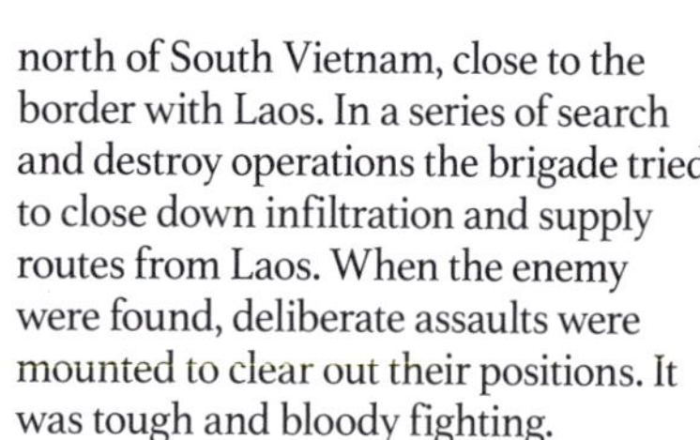

ABOVE: 101st Airborne troopers climbing through the devastated landscape on Hill 937 at Dong Ap Bia after the Battle of Hamburger Hill in May 1969.

in Saigon to clear the lower floors of the building of a detachment of Vietcong sappers.

A brigade of the 82nd Airborne Division was dispatched to South Vietnam in the aftermath of the 1968 Tet Offensive and remained in country for 22 months. The deployment was controversial when it emerged that most of the brigade's paratroopers had already served 12 month long tours in Vietnam in other units and were immediately returned home. As a result, it was converted into a light infantry brigade. The rest of the division remained in the United States, where it was called up to deal with urban riots and anti-war protests.

The Screaming Eagles of the 101st Airborne faced their toughest test in the spring of 1969 when they were dispatched to the A Shau Valley in the north of South Vietnam, close to the border with Laos. In a series of search and destroy operations the brigade tried to close down infiltration and supply routes from Laos. When the enemy were found, deliberate assaults were mounted to clear out their positions. It was tough and bloody fighting.

Hamburger Hill

During one operation in May 1969, the 3rd Battalion, 187th Infantry assaulted Dong Ap Bia Mountain, or Hill 937, where a strong North Vietnam unit was dug in. For 10 days, the paratroopers launched attack after attack on the enemy position but could only advance a few metres at a time. According to the 101st Airborne's official history: "the fighting on Hill 937 was some of the most brutal of the war and was often hand-to-hand."

The attackers had to fight through several defence lines, using grenades and trench clearing tactics. Despite hundreds of air strikes and artillery fire missions, the US advance was painfully slow. Reinforcements were called up including the 2nd Battalion, 501st Infantry, 1st Battalion, 506th Infantry and two companies of the 2nd Battalion, 506th Infantry. When journalists visited the battlefield and saw that the jungle canopy had been completely shredded by artillery fire

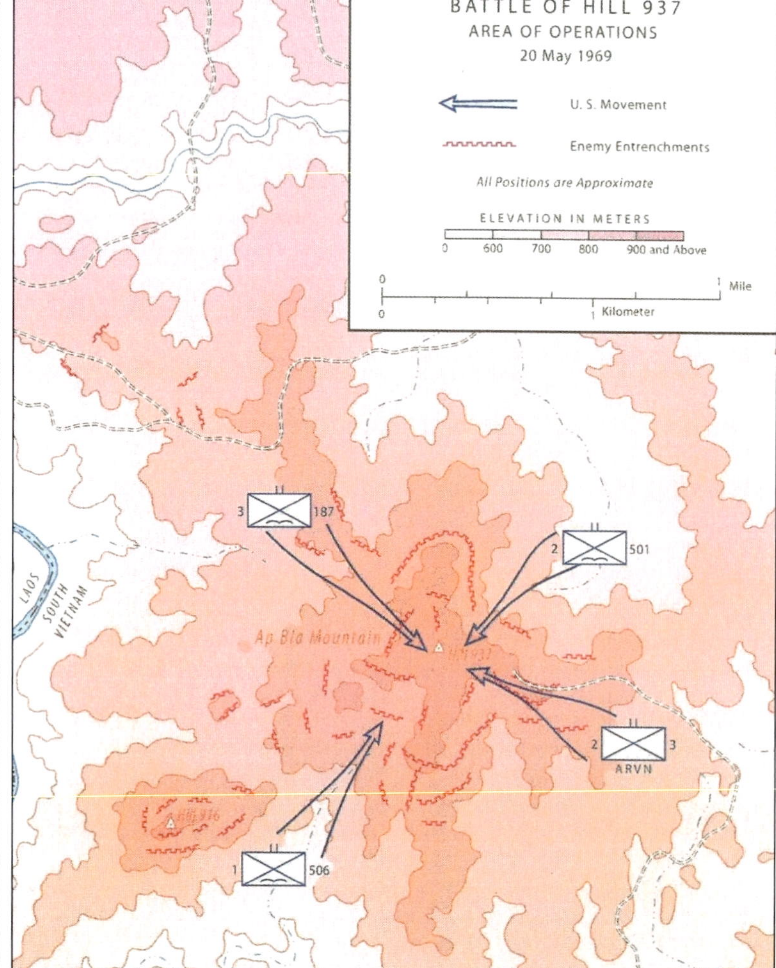

RIGHT: The Battle of Hill 937 – aka Hamburger Hill. (US ARMY CENTER OF MILITARY HISTORY)

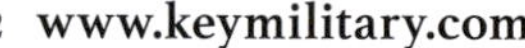

and airstrikes and Hill 937 was soon dubbed 'Hamburger Hill' because it looked akin to a meat grinder.

When the 101st Airborne were ordered to abandon the hill a day after its capture – for the loss of 72 dead and 372 wounded Americans - it came to epitomise the pointlessness of the US presence in Vietnam.

Defending the operation, the commander of the 101st Airborne, Major General John Wright, said that the hill's only significance was the fact that the enemy occupied it, saying: "My mission, was to destroy enemy forces and installations. We found the enemy on Hill 937, and that is where we fought them."

Following the A Shau Valley fighting the Screaming Eagles were pulled back for reorganisation and its aviation component expanded to make it a fully fledged airmobile division, akin to the 1st Cavalry. Now dubbed the 101st Airborne Division (Airmobile) it was to remain in Vietnam for nearly three more years. Its job was to cover the drawdown of US troops and hand over the war to the Saigon government, which was soon dubbed 'Vietnamization'. Orders from Washington were to minimise US casualties so the brunt of its operations in this period were carried out by its Bell AH-1G Cobra gunships and artillery, relegating its

paratroopers to guarding fixed fire bases and helicopter landing strips.

The division finally returned to its Fort Campbell home in May 1972. It was the last fully formed US division to serve in Vietnam. During their seven years in Vietnam, the 101st Airborne Division earned a reputation as an elite unit that could be relied on

in a crisis. According to the division's history, the North Vietnamese called the unit the 'Chicken Men' because of their insignia - the enemy Vietnamese had never seen an eagle before. Many enemy commanders warned their men to "avoid the Chicken Men at all costs because any engagement with them, they were sure to lose."

ABOVE: By the start of 1973 all US troops had left Vietnam and the Saigon government was on its own. Communist troops marched into Saigon in April 1975. (US ARMY)

LEFT: Members of the US Military Police keep back protesters during their sit-in at the Mall Entrance to the Pentagon during an anti Vietnam war protest in October 1967. The 82nd Airborne Division remained in the US for most of the Vietnam conflict to help contain growing protests and urban riots. (US ARMY)

Operation Urgent Fury

US Army Rangers capture Grenada's Airport, 1983

ABOVE: US Army Rangers had the task of seizing Grenada's main airport.
(US DOD)

During World War Two the US Army formed units called Rangers to conduct high risk raids into enemy territory. These were America's commandos. They achieved fame on D-Day when a daring Ranger unit scaled the cliffs under Pointe du Hoc in Normandy to capture a German gun battery.

After World War Two the Ranger units were disbanded as the US Army downsized into a peacetime organisation. Small Ranger companies were briefly reformed during the Korean and Vietnam conflicts for long reconnaissance and raiding missions. Their usefulness was recognised, and two Ranger battalions were formed in 1974 as part of the regular US Army. These new units were to be America's elite light infantry unit and they were trained and equipped to carry out lightning raids behind enemy lines.

A key mission for the Rangers was the capture of enemy airfields to allow follow on forces to flow in to establish a forward operating base. In this strategic insertion role, the Rangers were trained to land by parachute in surprise assaults. Every Ranger was trained to carry out low level mass combat parachute drops to a higher degree than mainstream paratroopers of the US Army's 82nd Airborne Division. In the early 1980s, the two Ranger battalions were held at a high level of readiness for global operations, often in support of classified special forces operations. The Rangers were dubbed 'the tip of the spear' and their officers proudly declared that their units were the best trained and equipped airborne battalions in the world.

So, when the government of the Caribbean island of Grenada was overthrown in a coup by pro-communist revolutionary factions in October 1983 it was not a surprise that the Rangers were put on alert to lead America's response. US President Ronald Reagan saw an opportunity to strike back at what he saw as a Moscow-backed revolution in America's backyard. The presence of several hundred American students on the island was a useful pretext for US intervention.

Urgent Fury

Orders were issued to the US Atlantic Command to pull together Operation

RIGHT: US President Ronald Reagan (second from left) was determined to overthrow Grenada's leftist government and install a regime friendly to the United States.
(WHITE HOUSE)

LEFT: **US satellite photographs of Port Salinas were some of the few pieces of intelligence available to the commanders of the Rangers sent to seize the airport.** (US DOD)

Urgent Fury, with the mission to seize control of the island from its revolutionary government and expel a contingent of Cuban military advisors and heavily armed 'construction workers'.

In less than a week troops were alerted, ships moved into position and aircraft redeployed to airfields within range of Grenada. A complex plan was to be executed on the early hours of October 25. US Marines would first land by helicopter around the coast of the island.

A key objective was to free the leaders of the Grenadian government who were being held by revolutionary militia fighters at Richmond Hill Prison and Fort Rupert. This was a job for the elite US Delta Force hostage rescue teams and the newly formed US Army 160th Special Operations Aviation Regiment (Airborne), which soon became known as the Nightstalkers. The rescue force took off from Barbados in daylight with the Delta Force troopers in five Sikorsky UH-60 Black Hawks and headed towards the prison. Intelligence had not detected the presence of several anti-aircraft guns around the site and as the strike force approached, the gunner began to

engage the American helicopters and the assault team had to circle, trying to find a suitable landing zone. One of the UH-60s was hit and crash landed, killing the pilot and three of the Delta Force operators.

As these initial operations were underway, US Air Force Lockheed MC-130E Combat Talons were leading a formation of C-130 Hercules to drop Rangers to seize the island's main airport at Port Salinas, which was ❯

BELOW: **US Air Force C-130 Hercules began landing at Port Salinas after its capture by the Rangers.** (US DOD)

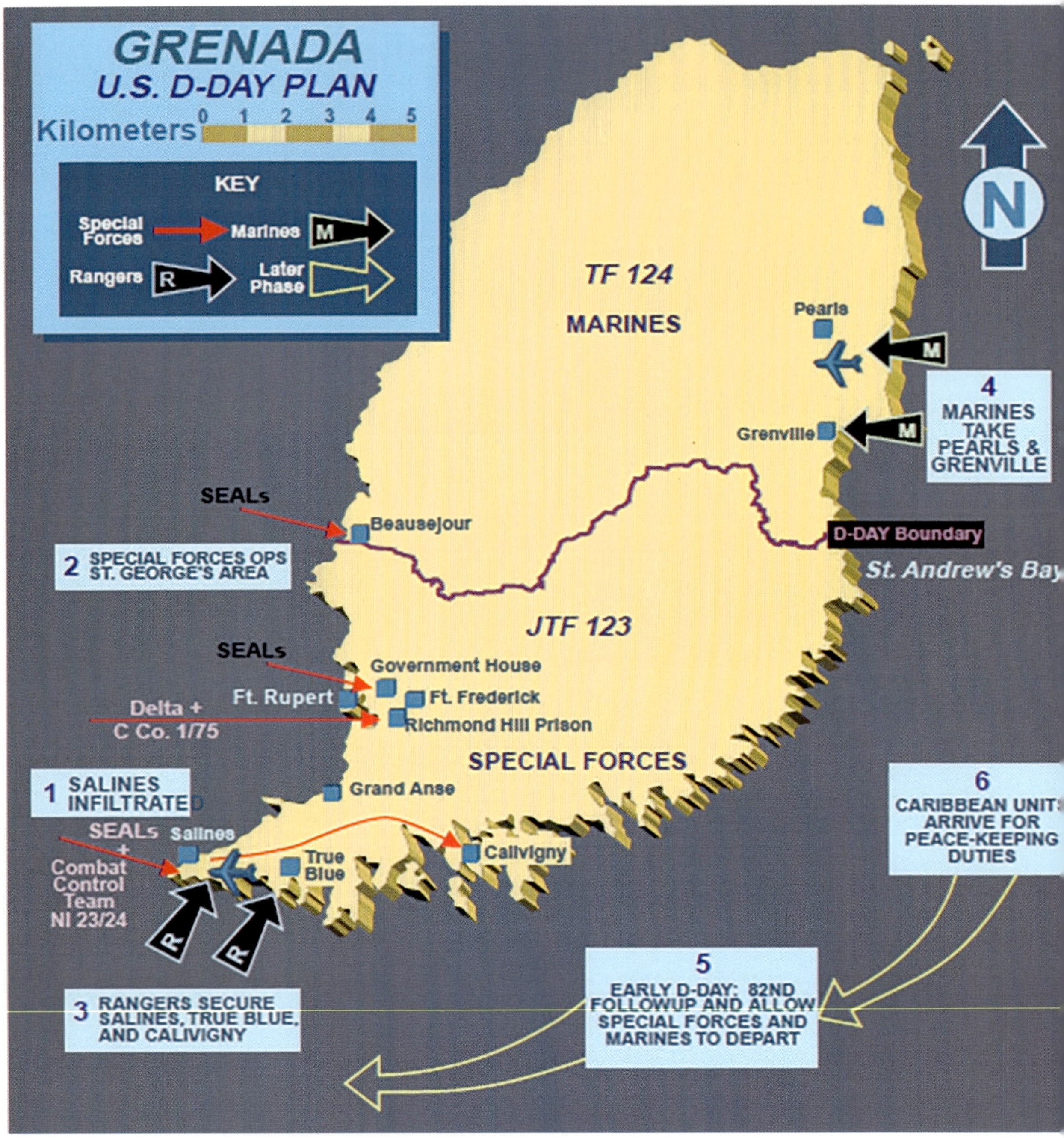

RIGHT: US D-Day Plan, Invasion of Grenada: Operation Urgent Fury. (US DOD)

BELOW: A second wave of troops from the 82nd Airborne Division landed at Port Salinas hours after Rangers had secured the airport. (US DOD)

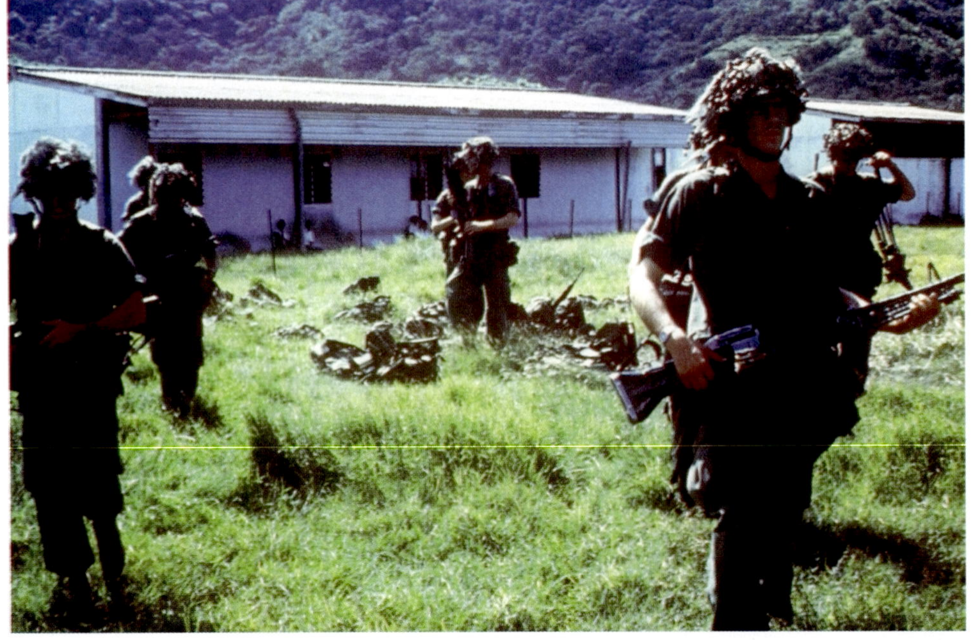

controlled by Cuban engineers. Once the airport was secured, the bulk of the 82nd Airborne Division was to fly into complete the US takeover of the island. This was to be the first US combat parachute drop since the Vietnam conflict and the most daring battalion-sized US parachute assault since World War Two.

During the early hours of October 25, the 1st and 2nd Battalions of the 75th Ranger Regiment loaded on board two MC-130Es and ten C-130s at Hunter Airfield in Georgia. The initial plan intended that one company of Rangers would jump onto the airfield to secure the airport's runway and allow the rest of the aircraft carrying the bulk of the force to land. Several aircraft contained heavily armed jeeps that were then to rapidly fan out from the airport and secure key objectives. There was little intelligence on the

state of defences around the airfield and although the plan called for the bulk of the force to land in C-130s, all the Rangers took their parachutes with them in case a jump insertion was needed.

Flying ahead of the transports was a Lockheed AC-130 Spectre gunship. These heavily armed aircraft were equipped with advanced night-vision systems and were given the mission of overflying the runway to check out if it was blocked to prevent landings. The main formation was staggered with two MC-130E and five C-130s carrying the 1st Battalion. They were followed by two more AC-130s and a final cell of five more C-130s carried the 2nd Battalion. The limited aircraft numbers meant each battalion could only take 250 Rangers with it for the initial drop.

A few minutes after arriving on station it was apparent to the Spectre crew that the runway was blocked by construction equipment and piles of building material. In the following wave of transport aircraft, Ranger commanders told their troops that the air landing operation was cancelled, and they had to rig for a combat parachute jump.

In the confined space of the aircraft, the Rangers rapidly donned their parachutes, grabbed extra ammunition from the jeeps and rigged their weapon containers. In peacetime this would have been done on the ground, with parachute

instructors checking to make sure all the troops had their chutes properly fitted. There was no time, and the Rangers used a buddy system to check each other's equipment. As it appeared the enemy were expecting an airborne attack, the decision was taken to reduce the jump height to 500 feet. This would minimise the time before the Rangers landed to less than 13 seconds, but it meant that there wouldn't be time to deploy a reserve parachute if the main one

failed. One of the battalions left its reserve chutes on the aircraft.

As the first cell of US aircraft approached the airfield the defenders opened fire with their anti-aircraft guns. The jump was temporarily aborted with minutes to go to allow the two AC-130s to fly forward and put the enemy anti-aircraft guns out of action. In the confusion one of the aircraft did not get the abort signal and dropped the command group – nearly 40 men - of the 1st Battalion

ABOVE: US troops spread out across Grenada to hunt down the remnants of the revolutionary regime and its militia forces. (US DOD)

BELOW: Soldiers and policemen from the Eastern Caribbean Defence Force were deployed to Grenada to assist US troops establish a new democratic government in Grenada. (US DOD)

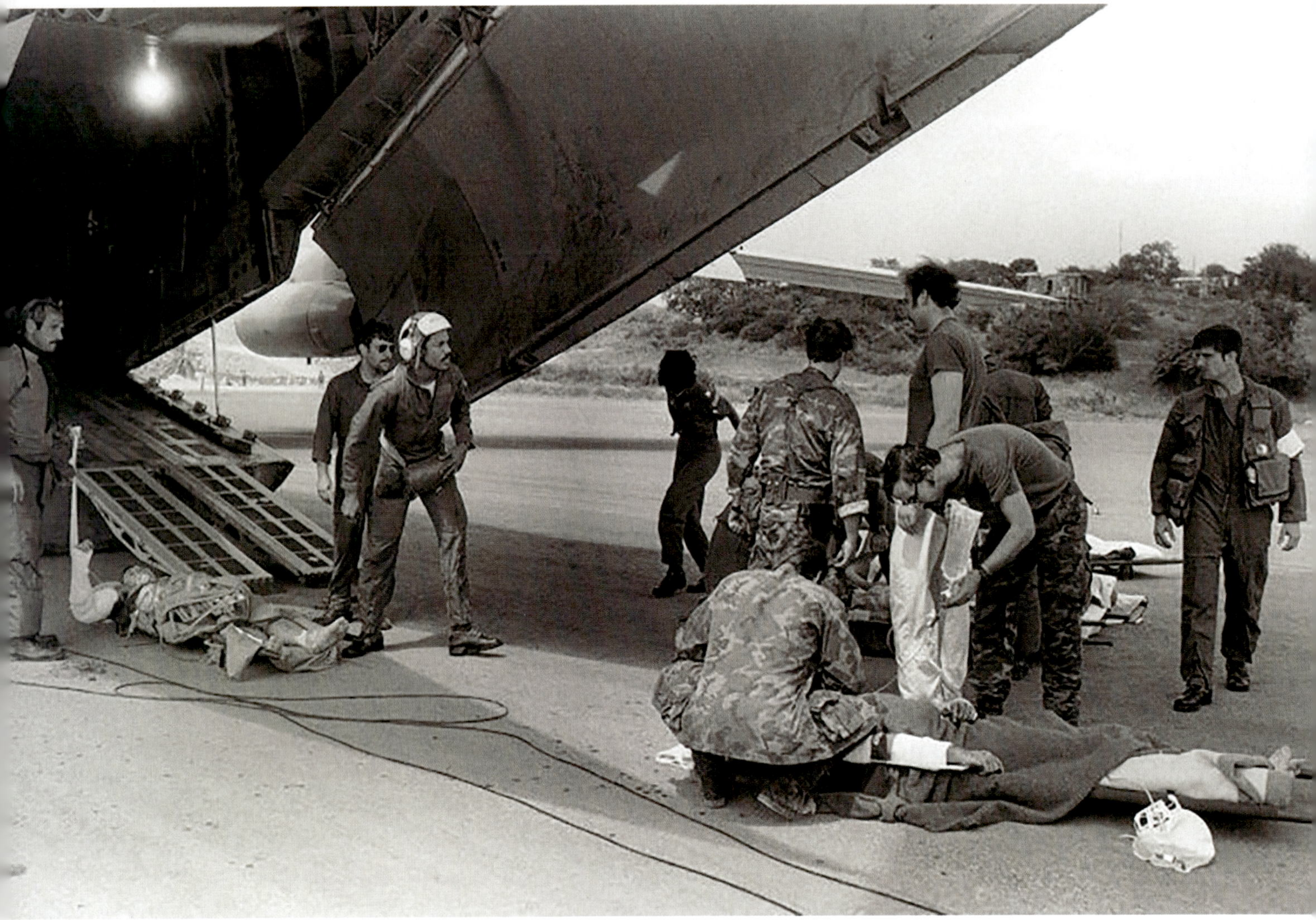

ABOVE: US Air Force C-141 Starlifters were sent to evacuate wounded US soldiers from Port Salinas airport. (US DOD)

as planned along the centre of the runway. They all landed safely and by just after 05:30am were taking up defensive positions.

The remainder of the US aircraft circled and returned once the AC-130s had finished taking out the anti-aircraft defences. It took nearly 90 minutes for the remaining aircraft to make their drop runs over the airport and for all the Rangers to get on the ground. Despite the frantic and chaotic change of plan to go a full parachute drop, all the Rangers landed safely, except for one who broke a leg on landing and one who got hung up when his static line became entangled. He was successfully dragged back onboard one of the Hercules.

Once on the ground, the Ranger commanders set some of their men to clear the runway to allow the 82nd Airborne to land. Troops 'hotwired' Cuban construction equipment to begin moving barricades and vehicles from the runway. While this was underway, Ranger companies began to engage groups of Cubans and local revolutionaries in the airport buildings and compounds on hills overlooking the runway. The defenders made only a token effort to resist after the Rangers called in more AC-130 strikes and then directed US Marine Corps Bell AH-1T helicopter gunships against a Cuban strong point. The Cuban troops started to surrender, and the revolutionaries began to withdraw.

A contingent of Rangers were dispatched to the True Blue university campus, just beyond the eastern edge of main runway, where hundreds of US students were believed to be located. The revolutionary militiamen guarding the campus fled when the Rangers approached and soon the US students were secured. Within hours they had been led onto the airfield to be flown to safety.

By 10am nine of the Hercules carrying the Ranger's armed jeeps were at last able to land and allow the US troops to begin pushing inland

RIGHT: Jeeps gave the US Army Rangers mobility to enable them to move out of Salinas airport. (US DOD)

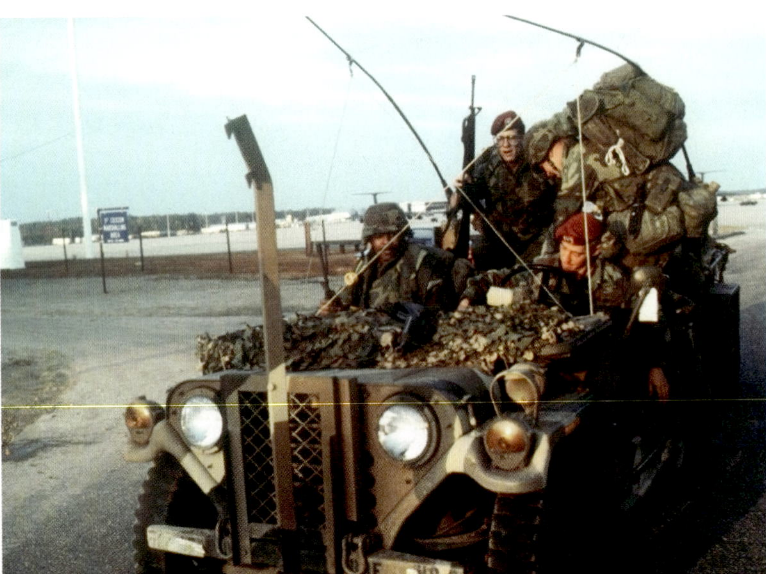

from the airport. Initial US losses were light but one of the Ranger jeeps was ambushed and its four crewmen killed.

Counter Attack

By the afternoon the revolutionaries had recovered from the shock of the US invasion and staged a counter attack against the Rangers. Three Soviet made BTR-60 wheeled armoured personnel carriers (APCs) led the attack on the US defences at the eastern edge of the airport. Rangers knocked out two APCs with hand held Light Anti-tank Weapon (LAW) rockets and an AC-130 finished off the third vehicle. The US hold on Port Salinas was now secure. The first of the Lockheed C-141 Starlifter aircraft carrying the 82nd Airborne came in to land and soon thousands of US paratroopers were on the ground and spreading out across Grenada to link up US Marines in the north of the island and Special Operations Forces in the capital, St Georges. The island's outnumbered military were soon overwhelmed, and President Reagan was able to claim victory.

The parachute assault by the Ranger battalions captured the strategic Port Salinas airfield in a matter of hours with only a handful of casualties. Despite the chaotic build-up to their jump, the Rangers displayed a huge

amount of 'airborne initiative' to adapt, improvise and overcome. As always in airborne operations, little went to plan, and the Rangers had to rapidly rethink their approach to overcome the resistance. Miraculously only one Ranger was injured in the jump and five Rangers were killed in the skirmishing around the airport later in the day. The AC-130 gunships proved decisive. This is a unique

capability that only the United States military possesses. Their range and endurance match that of the Hercules used to drop the Rangers, so they could easily accompany the main strike force and stay on station providing close air support.

The Ranger jump to capture Port Salinas airport is a classic example of a coup d'main operation by parachute to capture a strategic objective.

ABOVE: American students from the Saint George's University School of Medicine in Grenada held a press conference to thank the US military for their rescue. (US DOD)

BELOW: The success of the invasion of Grenada was a major boost to public support for the US military. US President Reagan hoped it would banish the 'ghost of Vietnam'. (US DOD)

Operation Desert Storm Air Assault

Iraq 1991

ABOVE: CH-47 Chinooks shuttled forward to deliver fuel, ammunitions, and spare parts to Objective Cobra to keep 101st Airborne Division's troops and helicopter gunships fighting inside Iraq. (US DOD/COMBAT CAMERA)

As dawn was breaking on February 24, 1991, more than 100 US helicopters lifted off from desert air strips and headed into Iraq. It was the biggest air assault operation ever attempted by the US Army. Swarms of attack helicopters and strike jets flew 'shotgun' ready to protect the troop carrying helicopters from Iraqi fire.

Crammed inside the Blackhawk and Chinook helicopters were hundreds of troopers from the US Army's 101st Airborne Division (Air Assault). They had spent days living in fox holes in the freezing Saudi desert and were raring to see action.

When the first helicopters touched down on an empty stretch of Iraqi desert, dubbed Objective Cobra, the airborne troopers spread out to set up a defensive screen to protect the next wave of helicopters. The helicopter pilots had GPS satellite navigation

RIGHT: General Norman Schwarzkopf devised the US offensive that devastated the Iraqi army occupying Kuwait. (US DOD/COMBAT CAMERA)

devices so the troops were dropped exactly in the right places. As more helicopters arrived, they started dropping off teams of engineers, helicopter mechanics and air traffic controllers. They set about building a series of forward arming and refuelling points. Within a matter of hours Objective Cobra was transformed into Forward Operating Base (FOB) Cobra and the 101st Airborne was ready to strike forward again. This was proving to be one of the best organised and expedited airborne operations in US military history.

The honour of firing the first shots of Operation Desert Storm famously fell to the Screaming Eagles two months earlier at 2.38am on January 17, 1999. For that mission eight McDonnell Douglas AH-6A Apache attack helicopters of the 1st Battalion, 101st Aviation Regiment had been accompanied by two US Air Force

Special Operations Sikorsky MH-5J Pave Low machines and headed out into the Iraqi desert before the war had officially begun. Task Force Normandy crossed the Iraqi border at low level and then headed 80 miles inside Saddam Hussein's country to attack two radar sites that covered a key section of air space. Coalition aircraft would then be able to penetrate deep into Baghdad undetected and take the Iraqi air defences around Baghdad by surprise.

The Pave Lows led the way using their satellite navigation system to lead the AH-64As to their targets and right on H-Hour, four of the Apaches blasted each radar site with their Hellfire missiles. In a sign of the times, video imagery of the strikes was recorded by the AH-64A's night-vision systems and later played to the media at a Pentagon press conference.

ABOVE: A 101st Airborne Division trooper cleans his M-16A2 rifle as he waits to board helicopters to fly into Iraq.
(US DOD/COMBAT CAMERA)

LEFT: An M-551 Sheridan light tank of the 82nd Airborne Division is loaded with supplies and waits to board a C-130 Hercules transport aircraft as part of the move of US airborne units into their attack position, ahead of the coalition ground offensive.
(US DOD/COMBAT CAMERA)

ABOVE: Troops from C Company, 1st Battalion, 187th Infantry, travel aboard an Air National Guard C-130 Hercules transport aircraft during the re-deployment of the 101st Airborne Division out into the Saudi desert, ahead of the move into Iraq. (US DOD/COMBAT CAMERA)

BELOW: General Schwarzkopf's plan to defeat the Iraqi army. (US DOD/COMBAT CAMERA)

The operation received significant publicity at the time. However, deep in the Saudi desert the remainder of the 101st Airborne was preparing to launch the world's largest ever air assault operation as part of the US Army's drive to defeat the 500,000 strong Iraqi army that had been occupying Kuwait since August 1990.

Stormin' Norman

The coalition commander, General 'Storming' Norman Schwarzkopf, devised an audacious plan to defeat the Iraqi army occupying Kuwait, as well as the armoured reserves of the Iraqi Republican Guard sitting back along the Kuwait-Iraq border. To paraphrase the head of the US Joint Chiefs of Staff, General Colin Powell, the idea was to 'cut off and kill' the Iraqi army. The 101st Airborne would spearhead this offensive.

The division had been preparing for this moment since it returned from Vietnam in 1972 and converted into the US Army's only air assault division. During the 1970s and 1980s,

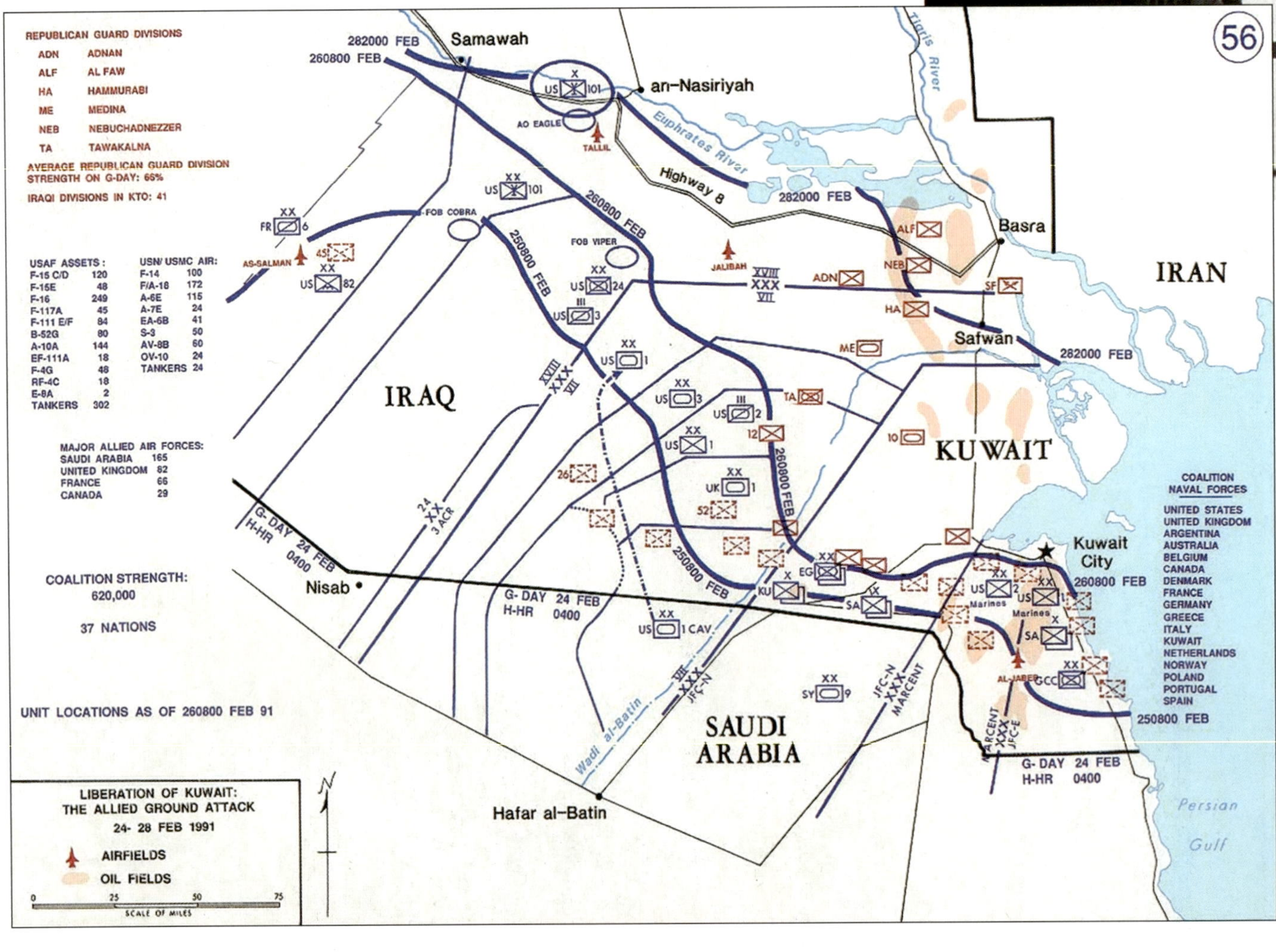

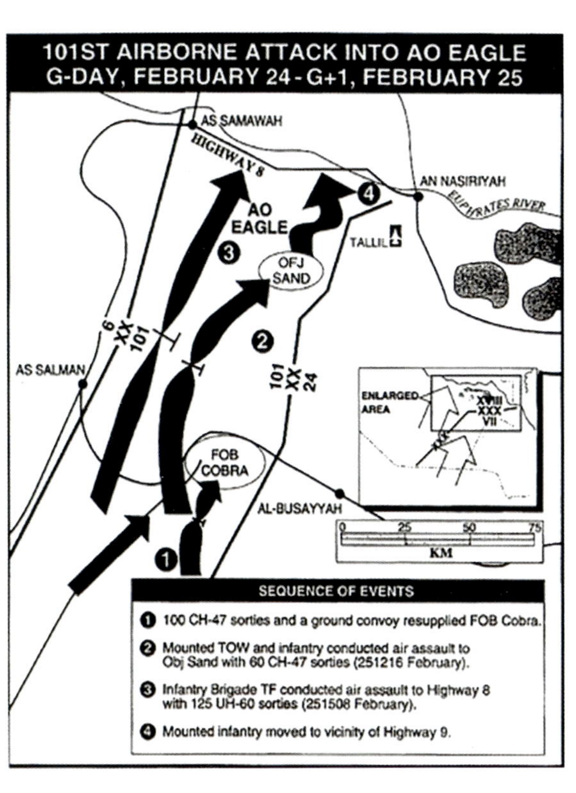

ABOVE: Waves of UH-60 Blackhawks lifted the first 101st Airborne Division troops into Iraq to seize Objective Rhino. (US DOD/COMBAT CAMERA)

BELOW: (US ARMY CENTER FOR MILITARY HISTORY)

the US Army had invested heavily in rotary wing hardware and developed a concept of operations – AirLand Battle – to integrate helicopters closely with ground units. AirLand Battle called for units, from battalions up to army corps to penetrate deep into the enemy's rear to surround and eventually destroy their main force. The concept envisaged helicopters being used to lift troops behind enemy lines, to move supplies forward to advancing ground units and destroy enemy armour with surprise missile attacks. Terrain, night, or severe weather would not provide the enemy with shelter or safe haven because of the widespread use of night-vision equipment, advanced radar sensors and electronic surveillance.

By 1990, each US Army division-sized formation had been provided with a combat aviation brigade with attack helicopters, troop, and cargo transport helicopters to enable it to put AirLand Battle into practice. Divisions also had a cavalry squadron for reconnaissance, which combined scouts equipped with both armoured vehicles and helicopters. Each corps headquarters was also provided with their own independent aviation brigades, which included two battalions of Apaches, to give corps commanders the ability to strike deep behind the front line at enemy second echelon forces. The US Army created a unique airmobile unit, the 101st Airborne Division (Air Assault), which was trained and equipped to conduct strategic helicopter operations far behind enemy lines.

When Iraqi troops rolled into Kuwait in August 1991, US President George HW Bush ordered 500,000 US troops to the region to counter the move by the Iraqi dictator, Saddam Hussein. Beginning on August 16, advanced elements of the 101st Airborne started to arrive in Saudi Arabia, which had been reinforced by additional Apache units from the 2nd Battalion, 299th Aviation Regiment, direct from its home garrison in Germany. The division's ◗

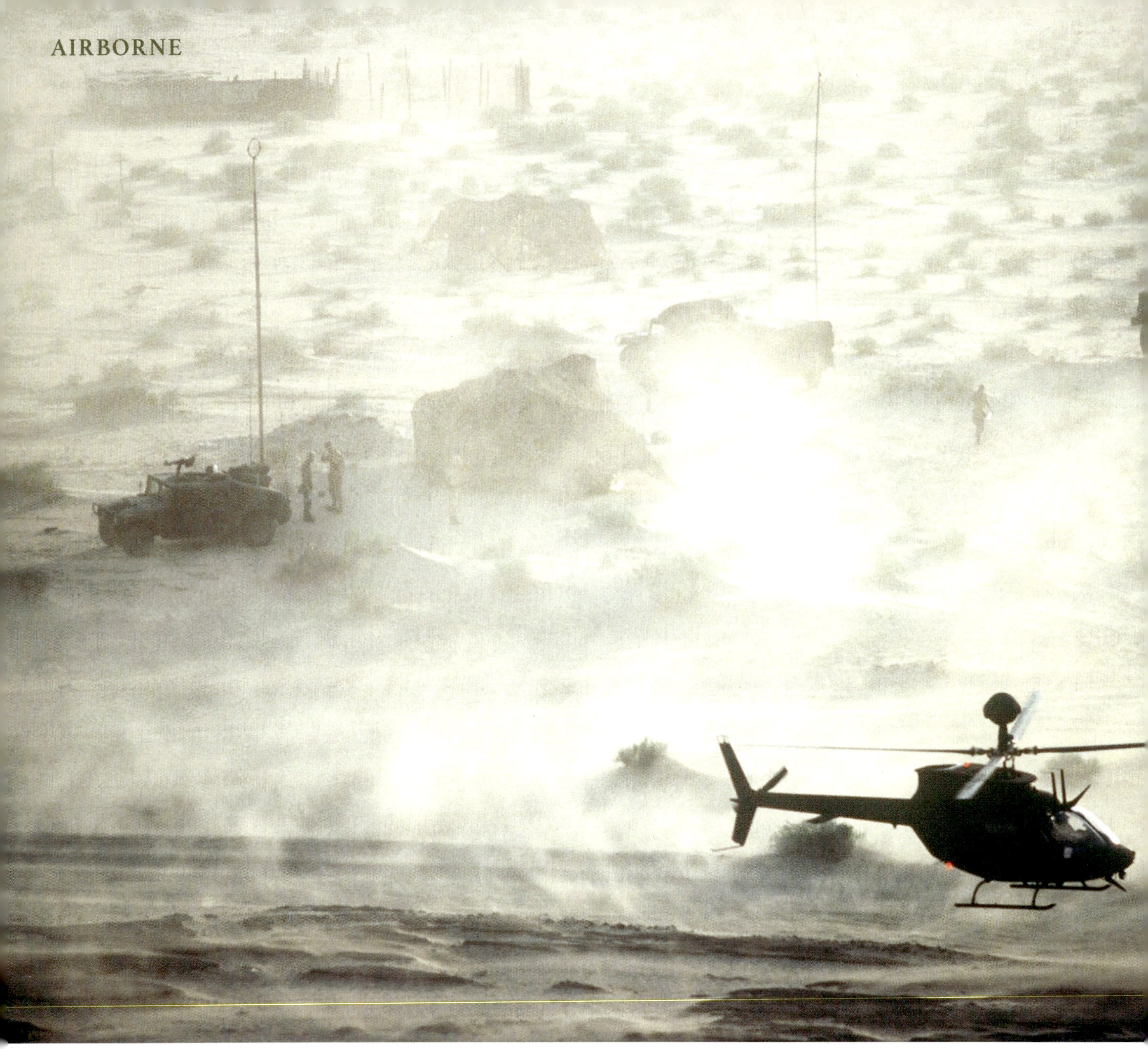

ABOVE: As VII Corps advanced, the 101st Airborne Division moved deeper into the Euphrates Valley to block the escape routes of the Iraqi Republican Guard. (US DOD/COMBAT CAMERA)

317 helicopters, including 36 Apache and 21 Bell AH-1F Cobras gunships, arrived by sea on US Navy fast transport ships and they soon moved up the coast to the 'Screaming Eagles' bases near the port of Damman.

By January 1991, diplomatic moves had failed to persuade Saddam Hussein to pull his troops out of Kuwait and President Bush ordered the launch of Operation Desert Storm on January 17 to drive Iraqi troops out of the oil rich emirate. The tanks of the US Army's VII Corps massed in the Iraqi desert to begin their outflanking move. Further out to the west the XVIII Airborne Corps, comprising the 101st and 82nd Airborne Divisions, as well as a French air mobile division, concentrated its helicopters at the airfield at Rafha and desert air strips.

To get the 101st Airborne into position to strike required a huge logistic operation, with road convoys of fuel tankers and ammunition trucks driving along desert roads to reach the assembly areas. The division's infantry units flew forward from their tented camps on the Saudi coast in shuttle flights of Boeing CH-47 Chinooks or US Air Force Lockheed C-130 Hercules to improvised desert air strips.

RIGHT: Cargo loads, including 105mm howitzers and their ammunitions, were positioned next to 101st Airborne Division's helicopter landing pads, ready to be hitched up to helicopters and flown into Iraq. (US DOD/COMBAT CAMERA)

Desert Bases

The 101st Airborne set up several FOBs in the desert and extensive

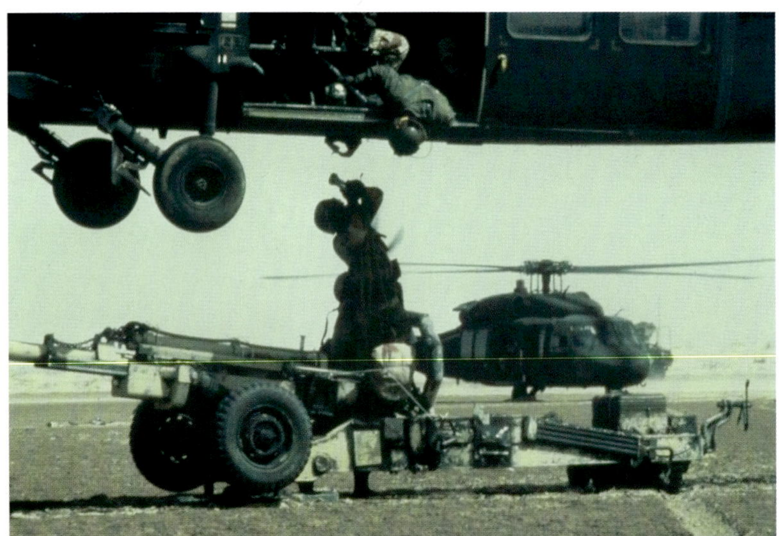

engineering support was needed to make them hospitable and operational. Makeshift revetments were created by bulldozing sand berms around helicopter dispersal areas, weapon dumps and fuel pillows. These desert bases were occupied until the start of the ground offensive when the US aviation brigades went into mobile mode and followed the armoured spearheads. Fuel tankers, ammunition trucks and command vans then moved behind the ground troops setting up forward air refuelling points (FARPs) and then leap frogged them forward as the advance continued.

101st Airborne troopers dug trenches and field fortifications around the FOBs. They were initially tasked to guard their bases and then get ready for the upcoming air assault operation. Rehearsals for the rapid loading of helicopters took place and cargo pallets of supplies positioned next to the helicopter landing pads. Several battalions were placed on alert, ready to go at a few hours notice in case the rapid deployment of troops was needed in response to unexpected events. Once the preparations were complete, the 101st Division just had to wait for the order to go. This was a far from pleasant experience. Temperatures dropped below zero at night, dust storms were common, and the US troops had little shelter beyond basic tarpaulin tents.

To close the ring around the Iraqis, XVIII Airborne Corps were

ABOVE: 105mm howitzers were flown forward to enhance the protection of 101st Airborne Division troops holding Objective Cobra. (US DOD/COMBAT CAMERA)

BELOW: (US ARMY CENTER FOR MILITARY HISTORY)

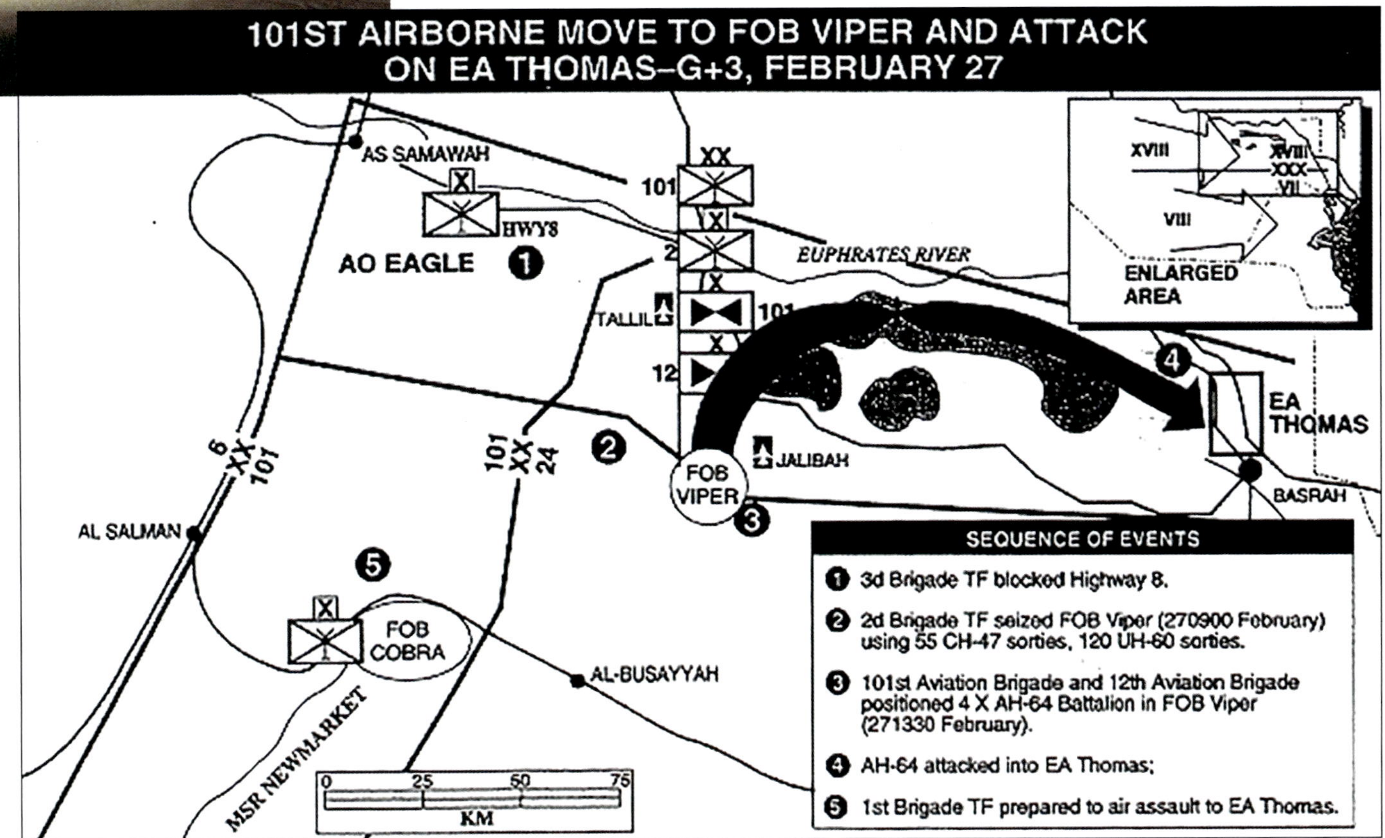

ABOVE: Huge quantities of equipment was abandoned by the retreating Iraqis, including Mi-24 attack helicopters. (US DOD/COMBAT CAMERA)

BELOW: A constant stream of helicopters delivered ammunition and supplies to the 101st Airborne Division at its bases deep inside Iraq. (US DOD/COMBAT CAMERA)

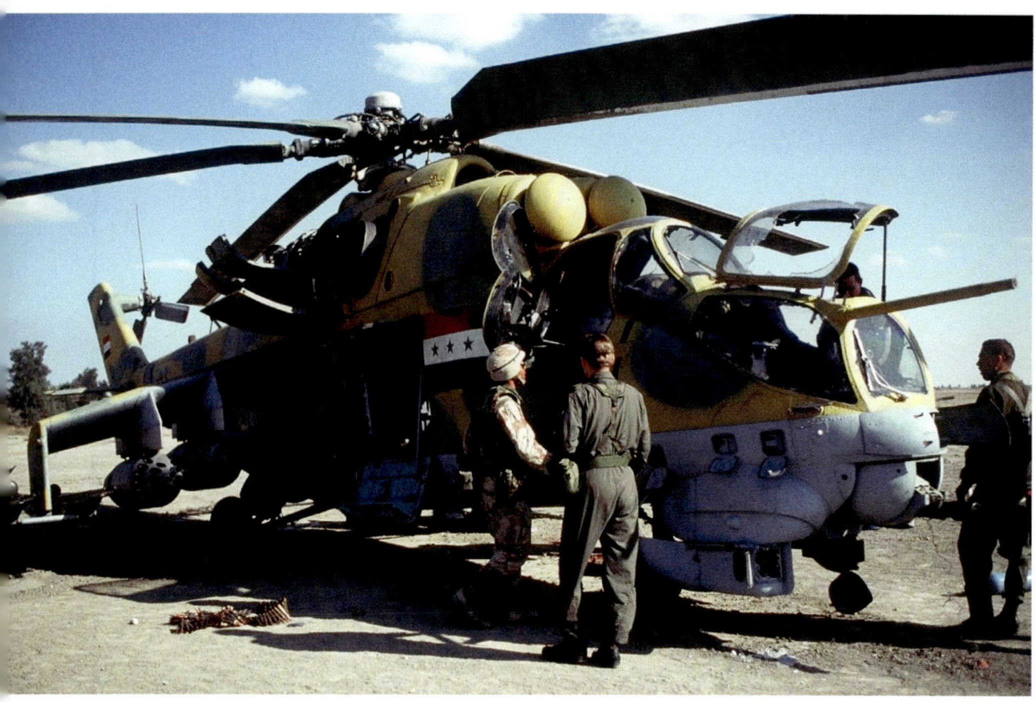

ordered to advance deep into the Iraqi army's rear area, using helicopters as its main means of transport. On February 14, reconnaissance missions started to fly deep into the Iraqi desert to try to pin point the main enemy positions. USAF Boeing B-52 Stratofortress heavy bombers were now carpet-bombing Iraqi positions on a daily basis. Iraqi morale was already starting to waiver in the face of this unrelenting pounding.

XVIII Airborne Corps helicopters were now criss-crossing the desert with regularity and in one famous incident on February 20, an entire Iraqi battalion tried to surrender to troops of the 101st Airborne's 1st Battalion, 187th Infantry Regiment. The battalion was scrambled after reports from the scout helicopters that had found the dejected Iraqis. Once its troops landed around the Iraqi position, the prisoners were all gathered together and evacuated on CH-47s back to a POW camp.

The US plan called for the XVIII Airborne Corps to leapfrog forward into the Euphrates valley, via several FOBs. To prevent surprises, small reconnaissance teams were landed by helicopters close to the proposed FOBs to ensure there were no Iraqi troops nearby, or to give warning of Iraqi threats in the area.

General Schwarzkopf set February 24 as G-Day, or Ground Day. At 7.25 am, the 101st Airborne's 1st Brigade lifted off on the first main attack of XVIII Airborne Corps' advance. A formation of 67 Sikorsky UH-60 Blackhawks, 30 Chinooks and Bell UH-1H Hueys headed 80 kilometres into Iraq and landed unopposed on a piece of empty desert, codenamed Objective Cobra.

USAF Fairchild A-10A Warthog ground attack jets and AH-1Fs escorted the transport helicopters as they flew north at low level. Before the air assault troops landed, the escorting strike jets and gunships started to bombard a small Iraqi infantry position two kilometres from Objective Cobra. An artillery battery was landed by Chinook, and it was soon in action against the Iraqi infantry. Within minutes of this bombardment starting the Iraqis surrendered to the circling AH-1Fs.

Feverish work now began to transform Objective Cobra into a fully

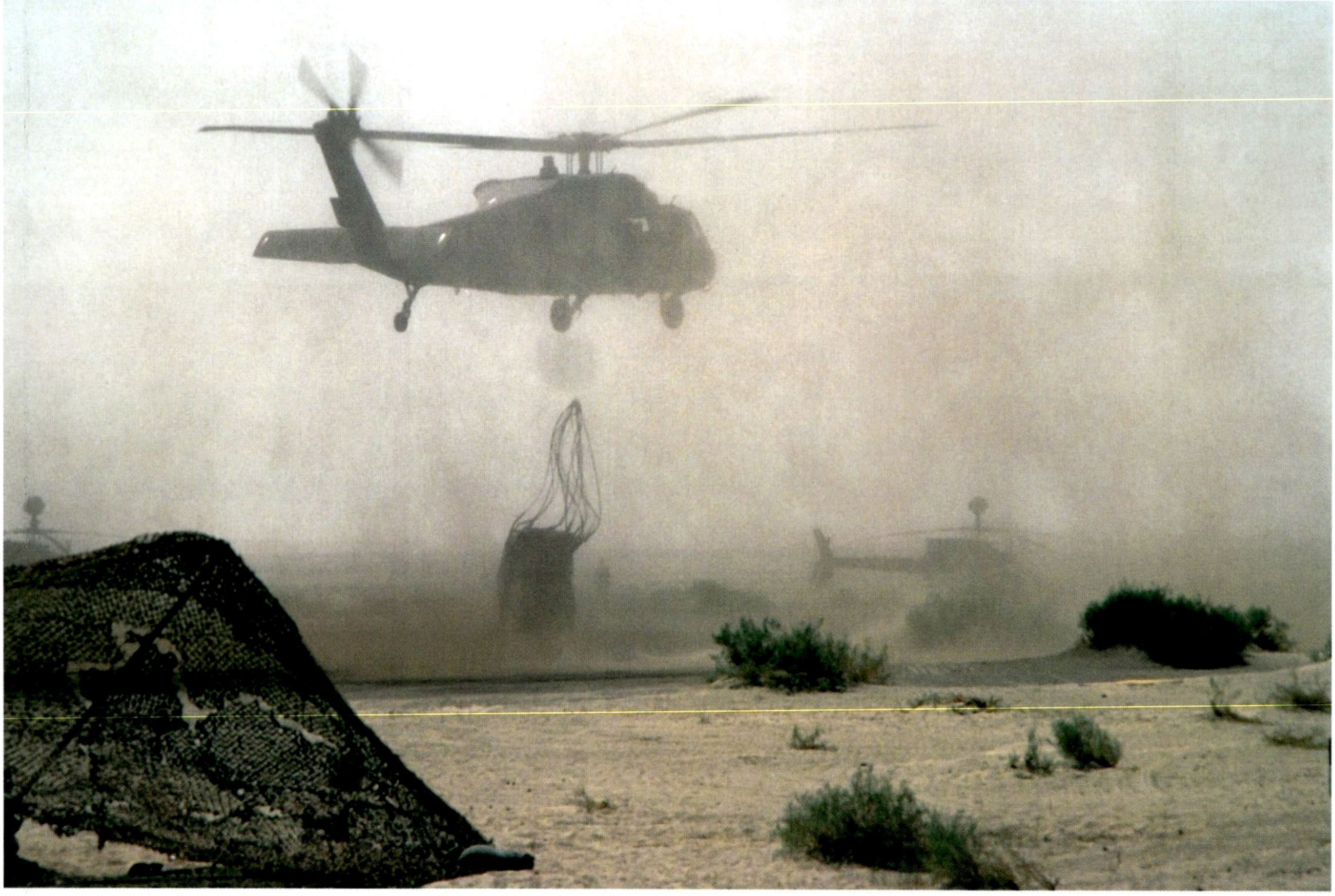

fledged FOB to enable the next phase of the operation to get underway. A shuttle of CH-47s, flying back and forth from Rafha airfield, brought in more troops, artillery, fuel, and ammunition. Soon the 101st Brigade had moved their Apache units up into Objective Cobra. They were rapidly re-armed, refuelled and set out to hunt for Iraqi tanks and artillery along the Euphrates Valley. Pairs of OH-58Ds patrolled the desert in every direction looking for targets and then calling up Apaches to hit them. Each Apache battalion established its own FARPs and began to rotate its companies through them so fully armed and fuelled AH-64As were always in the air, ready to strike.

By the afternoon of February 25, the 101st Airborne's 3rd Brigade was ready to launch on the next phase of the advance to the Euphrates. At 3pm, 66 UH-60s took off carrying 1,000 airborne troopers to seize five new FOBs near the town of Al Khibr on Highway 8, which linked the southern Iraqi city of Basra with Baghdad. By first light on February 26, the 3rd Brigade was firmly established, and US Army combat engineers were at work demolishing key road bridges to cut this key Iraqi supply route.

A huge dust storm engulfed southern Iraq on February 26, and soon 30kt winds had effectively grounded all of XVIII Airborne Corps' helicopters and its fixed wing air support. Fortunately, the Iraqi high command had little idea what the Americans were doing and there were no counter attacks to strike at the lightly armed units of the 101st Airborne.

Objective Viper

The weather cleared on February 27, and the 101st Airborne was able to launch three battalions of infantry aboard dozens of UH-60s to seize Objective Viper, 159 kilometres to the east of Objective Cobra. Apaches from the 101st and 12 Aviation Brigades escorted the air assault but there was no opposition. The only US casualties of the day were crew of a 101st Airborne medical evacuation UH-60 that was diverted to attempt to rescue a USAF Lockheed F-16 Fighting Falcon pilot who has been

shot down just behind enemy lines. The helicopter was shot down and five crew killed, three others were taken prisoner. Despite this setback, XVIII Airborne Corps and its two brigades of Apaches were now positioned deep behind enemy lines, ready to join the crucial battle that was looming over the next 24 hours as VII Corps engaged the Republican Guard.

Coming up behind the 101st Airborne were the tanks of the 24th Division, and by the early hours of February 27 they had driven across the desert to the Euphrates valley.

While the bulk of XVIII Airborne Corps headed east to join the battle with the Republican Guard, its western flank was protected by the French Daguet (Dagger) Division and the US 82nd Airborne Division. To clear the way the 82nd Airborne's two Apache battalions, backed by USAF jets, staged a strike on Iraqi tanks and artillery defending As Salman airbase on the night of February 18. More strike missions followed during the following day as the Apaches bombarded the Iraqi division spread out between the airbase and the Saudi border.

When the Daguet Division's armoured columns crossed the border, French army Aerospatiale Gazelles flew at low level ahead

of them. Formations of 30 French helicopters swarmed over the desert engaging any Iraqi positions they encountered with HOT wire guided missiles. During the advance the French helicopters knocked out 127 tanks, vehicles, and bunkers. By the time the French Foreign Legion drove through the gates of As Salman airbase, the Iraqi 45th Division had ceased to exist as a fighting force. The French troops and the US 82nd Division spent the rest of the war rounding up prisoners.

With the calling of the ceasefire on the morning of February 28, US and coalition units halted their advance. The Iraqi army had been devastated by the coalition air offensive and the lighting advance during the '100 Hour' ground war. Iraq was now engulfed in revolution and Saddam Hussein tried to re-organise his shattered army to protect his regime.

The 101st Airborne Division's rampage across the desert of southern Iraq was the largest air assault operation in military history, with more than 300 helicopters delivering thousands of US troops deep behind Iraqi lines. The insertion of the US air assault troops cut off one of the main Iraqi escape routes from Kuwait and channelled Saddam Hussein's troops onto the guns of the US VII Corps tanks.

ABOVE: When the ceasefire was called 101st Airborne Division troops began inspecting the devastation they had unleashed on the Iraqi army. (US DOD/COMBAT CAMERA)

BELOW: In the days after the ceasefire there were so many Iraqi troops surrendering that the 101st Airborne Division stopped trying to take them into custody and just told them to walk home. (US DOD/COMBAT CAMERA)

SUBSCRIBE

TO YOUR FAVOURITE MAGAZINE

AND SAVE

Officially The World's Number One Military Aviation Magazine...
Published monthly, AirForces Monthly is devoted entirely to modern military aircraft and their air arms. It has built up a formidable reputation worldwide by reporting from places not generally covered by other military magazines. Its world news is the best around, covering all aspects of military aviation, region by region; offering features on the strengths of the world's air forces, their conflicts, weaponry and exercises.

key.aero/airforces-monthly

America's Best-Selling Military Aviation Magazine
With in-depth editorial coverage alongside the finest imagery from the world's foremost aviation photographers, Combat Aircraft is the world's favourite military aviation magazine. With thought-provoking opinion pieces, detailed information and rare archive imagery, Combat Aircraft is your one-stop-source of military aviation news and features from across the globe.

key.aero/combat-aircraft

Operation Telic

Britain's 16 Air Assault Brigade in Iraq 2003

A patrol of 16 Air Assault Brigade's Pathfinder Platoon had passed through American lines en route to Qalat Sakir airfield. The airfield was the target of a major air assault operation by the brigade and the Pathfinders were to help secure it. As they drove through the night, Iraqi Fedayeen fighters in pick-up trucks opened fire on the British troops and tried to block their escape route. Sergeant Nathan Bell led his patrol off into the desert to escape the attention of the Iraqi militiamen and manning the general purpose machine gun in the front of his vehicle, Bell shot up several Iraqi positions as they headed south towards friendly forces. For his bravery that night, Bell was awarded the Military Cross.

The incident was one of many involving troops of the British Army's elite airborne force, 16 Air Assault Brigade. It is the modern successor to the 1st and 6th Airborne Divisions of World War Two fame and 16 Independent Parachute Brigade that landed at Suez. It was formed in 1999 to be Britain's dedicated air manoeuvre force that would use aircraft and helicopters both to deploy strategically to overseas crisis zones and then to move around complex battlefields. Under its air manoeuvre concept, 16 Brigade's troops would use aviation to both move and to fight. Aircraft and helicopters would give it agility. This would compensate for a lack of tanks and heavy artillery available to British Army armoured and mechanised brigades.

The brigade had been deployed on a peacekeeping mission to Macedonia in 2001 and then a few months later to Kabul in Afghanistan. So, when the brigade was sent to Kuwait to join the build up of British troops preparing to invade Iraq in the first weeks of 2003, it would be its first test in large scale conventional combat operations.

The brigade was led by Brigadier Jonathan 'Jacko' Page, who had commanded a platoon of 2 PARA during the 1982 Falklands war and then a tank squadron in the 1991 Iraq war. He was considered the most innovative tactician ever to have commanded 16 Brigade. As it turned out he would need this ability to innovate and improvise because 16 Brigade's mission kept changing throughout its deployment to Iraq.

Desert Deployment

Once 16 Brigade got the word to deploy on January 20, 2003, its 1,800 vehicles, cargo containers and 22 Army Air Corps (AAC) helicopters

ABOVE: Burning Iraqi oil wells lit up the night sky as 16 Air Assault Brigade moved into Iraq in March 2003. (MOD/CROWN COPYRIGHT)

LEFT: Iraq in 2003. (US CIA)

ABOVE: RAF Chinooks were on alert for several days to be ready to fly 16 Air Assault Brigade's paratroopers deep behind Iraqi lines to capture Qalat Sakir airfield. (MOD/CROWN COPYRIGHT)

were loaded onto cargo ships for the three week long voyage to Kuwait.

The brigade deployed to Kuwait with 1st and 3rd Battalion, The Parachute Regiment (1 & 3 PARA), 1st Battalion, The Royal Irish Regiment in the air assault role and 3 Regiment AAC, which was designated an aviation battlegroup. The Parachute Regiment and the Royal Irish battalions each mustered around 700 soldiers, equipped as light role infantry.

In addition to their infantry, the three battalions boasted support companies, containing 81mm mortar, general purpose machine gun, Milan anti-tank guided missile, sniper, reconnaissance, and assault pioneer platoons. These platoons were all mounted in Land Rover or Pinzgauer 4 x 4 vehicles and provided their battalions with hard hitting mobile strike forces, dubbed Mobile Support Groups (MSGs) to spearhead the

invasion of Iraq. These highly mobile units drew their inspiration from the World War Two long range desert group patrols that packed heavy fire power with high speed desert mobility.

1 PARA was designated as an airborne task force (ABTF), and it took all its parachutes and drop equipment to Kuwait. A detachment of four RAF Lockheed C-130 Hercules transport aircraft deployed to a US Marine Corps airstrip in the Kuwaiti desert to ready to launch the ABTF into action if needed.

The Brigade's Offensive Support Group (OSG) contained the bulk of its long range fire power, including four batteries of 105mm Light Guns belonging to 7th Parachute Regiment Royal Horse Artillery (7 RHA). 7 RHA's

control teams of Forward Observer Officers (FOO) and forward air controllers (FACs) went looking for targets in heavily armed Land Rovers. 16 Brigade also contained two specialist reconnaissance units that were optimised and trained to call down artillery fire and air strikes. The Pathfinder Platoon was a 40-strong group of reconnaissance specialists also mounted in heavily armed Land Rovers. D Squadron, The Household Cavalry (HCR), was the only armoured unit assigned to 16 Brigade. It had 20 Scimitar Combat Reconnaissance Vehicle (Reconnaissance) (CVR(T)) lightly armoured scout vehicles which had specialist night-vision equipment fitted.

All of 7 RHA's gun batteries, along with all 16 Brigade's artillery observers and FACs were connected to the central

BELOW: Dispatch riders from 216 Signals Squadron speed across the Iraqi desert to deliver documents to units of 16 Air Assault Brigade. (MOD/CROWN COPYRIGHT)

firepower control centre within 16 Brigade's headquarters so artillery and air support could be rapidly massed against targets.

Oil Fields

The Scimitars of the Household Cavalry crossed into Iraq during the evening of March 21 to link up with the US 5th Marine Regiment, which had secured the Rumalyah oil field complex, just over the border. The US Marines had swiftly overwhelmed Iraqi resistance. They handed over control of the oil fields to 16 Brigade and then rapidly headed north towards Baghdad.

Preparations were accelerated for a mission to seize Qalat Sakir airbase in southeast Iraqi using a helicopter and air drop operation by 1 PARA. Eight RAF Boeing Chinook HC2 heavy lift helicopters were allocated for the mission and US Marine AH-1W Cobra helicopter gunships were to fly close escort for the RAF helicopters to neutralise any threats to the mission.

While 16 Brigade was mopping up in the Rumalyah oil fields, the tanks of the British 7 Armoured Brigade were moving towards the outskirts of Basra and the US Marines were approaching Nasiriyah. Iraqi forces in both of these cities were now starting to put up serious resistance.

For 16 Brigade, this meant that its air manoeuvre operation to Qalat Sakir was on put on hold to allow the British to concentrate on reducing resistance in Basra. For five days 1 PARA sat in its assembly area waiting to get the order to launch the Qalat Sakir strike before the operation was cancelled by the government in London.

On the morning of March 26, it was back on, to be launched the

following evening. US Marine Corps McDonnell Douglas F/A-18D Hornets carried out reconnaissance flights over the airfield and reported the presence of Iraqi anti-aircraft missile batteries. At the Joint Helicopter Force (JHF) base in Kuwait the reports caused considerable unease among the RAF Chinook and US Marine Cobra pilots. They estimated at least one Chinook would be shot down, with the loss of dozens of paratroopers. The operation was placed on temporary hold again as senior commanders debated what to do. By the late afternoon, it was back on, and the operation was scheduled for that evening. Just as darkness was falling news came in that the US Marine Corps refuelling point outside Nasiriyah, where the helicopter force needed to refuel, was under sustained Iraqi artillery and mortar fire. The troops and helicopter crews were stood down again. A few hours later, US Marine Corps troops heading for Baghdad approached Qalat Sakir from the south and found it undefended - 16 Brigade's Qalat Sakir mission was cancelled and would never be resurrected.

One consequence of the Qalat Sakir operation were the events recounted at the beginning of this section. G (Mercer's Troop) Battery of 7 RHA had been moving by road via Nasiriyah to support the assault on the airfield when it got caught up in heavy street fighting in the city between US Marines and Fedayeen fighters loyal to the Baghdad regime.

The Pathfinders had also been ordered to move by road, via Nasiriyah, but importantly they got through the town before the Iraqis

ABOVE: The Iraqi desert was unforgiving, and 16 Air Assault Brigade's troops had to learn to survive and fight in this environment. (MOD/CROWN COPYRIGHT)

started to put up major resistance. They started to drive north towards Qalat Sakir and ran into the group of Fedayeen fighters which resulted in the action that led to Sgt Nathan Bell's Military Cross.

With its air assault operation cancelled, 16 Brigade was now ordered to focus on containing the Iraqi 6th Armoured Division, that was based in a marshy region to the northwest of Basra city. The HCR, Pathfinders, MSG of 3 PARA and Westland Lynx AH7 armed helicopters of 3 Regiment Army Air Corps were ordered to probe north to find the centre of Iraqi resistance and call down artillery fire and air strikes.

For over a week this battle grew in intensity as 16 Brigade pushed its reconnaissance forces into the battle by helicopter or ground movement. Around the clock, these small reconnaissance teams were calling ▶

BELOW: The Household Cavalry Regiment linked up with the US Marine Corps in the early hours of the war to allow the American force to head north to Baghdad. (MOD/CROWN COPYRIGHT)

down artillery fire from 7 RHA's guns against Iraqi bunkers and tanks. Then 3 Regiment's Lynx helicopters joined the battle, engaging targets with TOW missiles or calling in artillery fire.

This was by no means a one sided battle, with the Iraqis returning plenty of artillery fire. For 16 Brigade's artillery spotters and forward air controllers the attention of Iraqi artillery was a constant danger, and the best defence was a rapid withdrawal out of range in their vehicles, before they would re-group and try to find another way to approach their targets. The British reconnaissance teams often dismounted to move forward to occupy covert observation posts to watch their Iraqi opponents for days on end, relying on secrecy for protection.

Deadly Game

In effect, a few hundred members of 16 Brigade were playing a deadly game of cat and mouse with several thousand Iraqi defenders, who had by no means given up the fight.

The Iraqis were firing back with their South African made G5 155mm howitzers which outranged 7 RHA's 105mm guns so the regiment staged a series of artillery raids. The regiment's 105mm batteries were raced forward to firing points to engage the Iraqis before they rapidly withdrew when it was feared the Iraqis had identified their positions and were directing artillery fire against them.

During this period, the bulk of 16 Brigade's infantry units were not engaged en masse and stood guard on the Rumalyah oil fields so the bulk of the action was controlled by the OSG.

The Pathfinder Platoon was now inserted deep behind Iraqi lines by RAF Chinooks to watch routes towards Baghdad that the commander of US Marines was considering using. The teams were successfully extracted and were debriefed by senior US Marine Corps officers before the big US attack on Baghdad.

On April 6, US troops entered Baghdad and orders were given for the tanks of 7 Brigade to sweep into Basra, with 1 PARA in support. The old kasbah district of the city was 1 PARA's objective and the Paratroopers moved forward expecting to meet heavy resistance. However, the advance proved an anti-climax with cheering crowds of locals filling the streets to welcome the British troops. The Fedayeen were long gone.

With the overt fighting over, British troops were assigned responsibility for securing the southeast of Iraq and they were ordered to move quickly to establish control of all major towns in Maysan province, which had a population of over a million people.

The precarious situation in southern Iraq was amply demonstrated on June 24, when troops of the 1 PARA battlegroup came under attack in Majar-al-Kabir, to the south of Al Amara. A patrol of Paratroopers came under attack on the outskirts of the town, while inside the town's police station six Royal Military Policemen (RMP) were killed by a mob of tribesmen. Communications problems and limited intelligence gathering capabilities were all identified as contributing to this tragedy by a subsequent army board of inquiry.

In the course of this battle 16 Brigade's air manoeuvre tactics claimed the destruction of 86 Iraqi tanks and scores of enemy artillery pieces, effectively neutralising the Iraqi 6th Armoured Division at a crucial point in the war. 16 Brigade lost 11 dead during the battle for Iraq. One solider died in friendly fire, two were lost in road accidents, one when children accidently set off some abandoned ordnance, one to a suspected negligent discharge of a weapon, and the six RMPs in the Majar-al-Kabir incident.

ABOVE: Eighty-six Iraqi tanks were destroyed by 16 Air Assault Brigade during its battles in Iraq. (TIM RIPLEY)

LEFT: Once the fighting died down British paratroopers were sent into Iraqi towns and villages to win hearts and minds as the war drew to a close. (MOD/CROWN COPYRIGHT)

Battle for the Platoon Houses

Helmand Province, Afghanistan 2006

ABOVE: The Paratroopers of 16 Air Assault in Helmand during 2006 found themselves in most intense fighting experienced by the British Army since the Korean War of the 1950s. (MOD/CROWN COPYRIGHT)

While Britain sweltered in the long hot summer of 2006, British paratroopers found themselves besieged in several small bases across Afghanistan's Helmand province.

Thousands of heavily armed guerrilla fighters of the Taliban bombarded the British bases, dubbed 'Platoon Houses', around the clock and regularly tried to storm the isolated outposts.

The troops trapped in these bases relied on British helicopters to deliver food, water, and ammunition to keep them fighting and to evacuate their wounded. If the Taliban surged forward, then waves of Royal Air Force Harrier jump jets or Army Air Corps (AAC) Westland Apache AH1 gunships would be needed to keep the enemy at bay. Without their aerial lifeline, the paratroopers would not have been able to hold out.

When Britain's Defence Secretary, Dr John Reid announced 16 Air Assault Brigade's mission to Afghan in January 2006, he had described it as a peacekeeping operation. It would be focused on delivering humanitarian aid and undertaking reconstruction efforts to improve the lot of Helmand's impoverished population. A few weeks later he made his much quoted comment that he hoped British troops would "not fire a shot" during their new mission.

The British force deploying to Helmand as part of an expansion of the NATO footprint in southern Afghanistan would involve 3,500 troops of 16 Brigade. Its core infantry combat unit was 3rd Battalion, The Parachute Regiment (3 PARA), led by Lieutenant Colonel Stuart Tootal, and it would for the first time see the deployment of AAC Apache attack helicopters.

The Triangle

16 Brigade's commander, Brigadier Ed Butler, was no stranger to Afghanistan having led 22 Special Air Service (SAS) Regiment into the country in 2001. The main effort of the UK's Helmand Task Force would be to secure what become known as the 'triangle' between the provincial capital Lashkar Gar, the northern town of Gereshk and the soon to be built British base out in the desert known as Camp Bastion. Only once the 'triangle' was secure and

RIGHT: Brigadier Ed Butler led 16 Air Assault Brigade in its battles in Helmand province in the summer of 2006. (TIM RIPLEY)

development projects well underway would UK troops transition to a more offensive mode to launch 'search and destroy' missions in remote regions against small groups of Taliban. This first phase was expected to last months rather than weeks.

Even before Brigadier Butler had deployed all his troops in May 2006, the Taliban had moved to prevent the entry of the British force into Helmand. The first phase of the Taliban offensive was against a small contingent of French and US Special Forces training locally recruited Afghan National Army (ANA) troops near the Kajaki Dam in the far north of Helmand province. Fear of the sudden arrival of hundreds of Taliban, led the handful of French and American troops to form up their Afghan allies in a convoy of trucks and head south to the NATO base outside Sangin on May 20. The convoy had barely gone a few kilometres when it was ambushed. Hundreds of

LEFT: RAF Chinook heavy lift helicopters were central to 16 Air Assault Brigade's operations in Helmand province, flying paratroopers on offensive operations and keeping the Platoon Houses supplied. (MOD/CROWN COPYRIGHT)

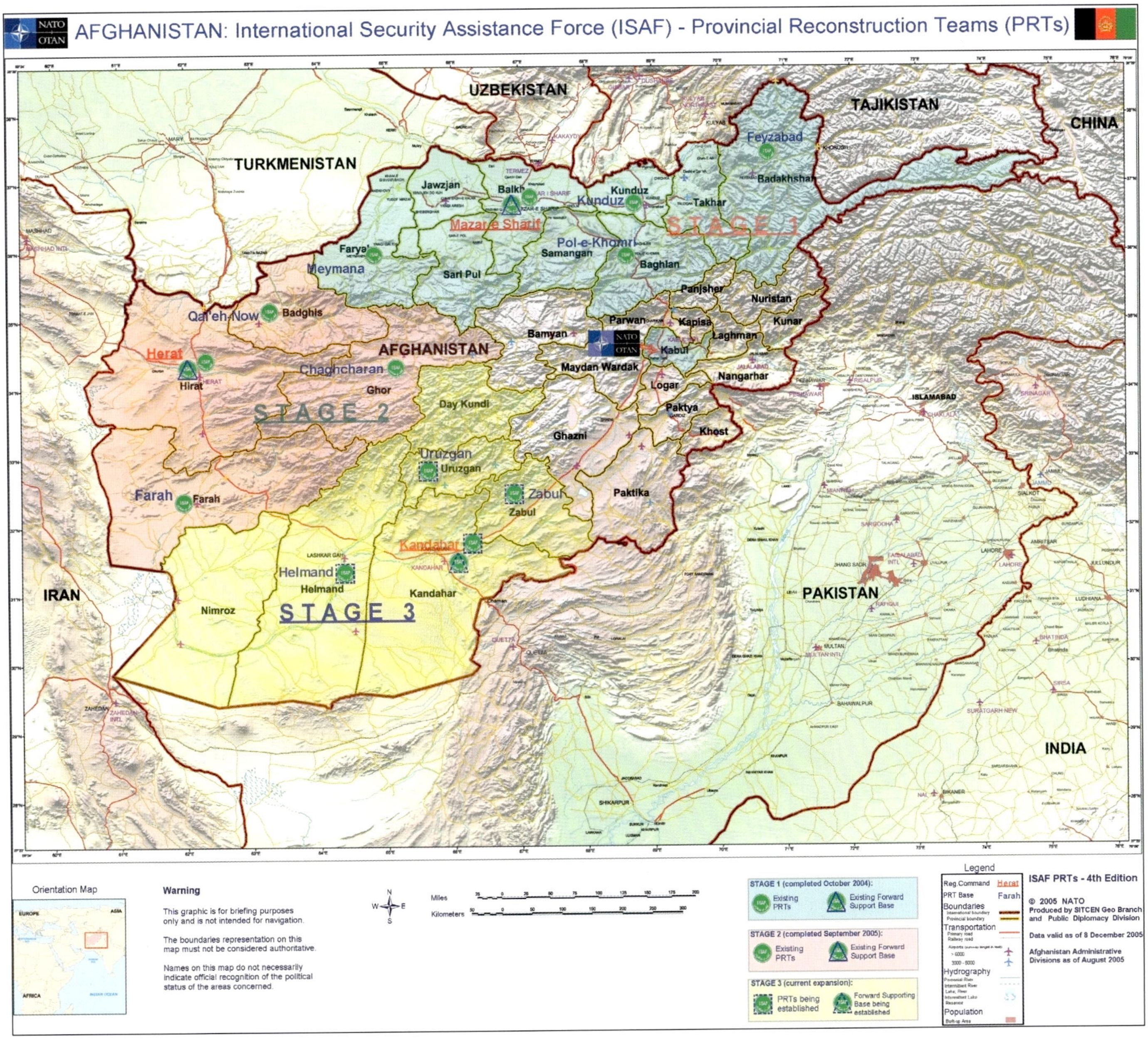

Taliban and their local allies subjected the convoy to a sustained attack over several dozen miles of road.

In Lashkar Gar, Governor Mohammad Daud was by now in a panic. The Taliban appeared to be rolling across northern Helmand unopposed. He turned to British and demanded that they help stop the Taliban offensive. Government compounds, known as district centres, in Musa Qalah, Now Zad, Sangin, and Baghran appeared about to fall, or so said Daoud. Butler conferred with senior British, NATO and US officers in Kabul, as well as with the Ministry of Defence in London, about what to do.

BELOW: The British move into Helmand province was part of NATO's plan to establish alliance troops and bases across Afghanistan. (NATO)

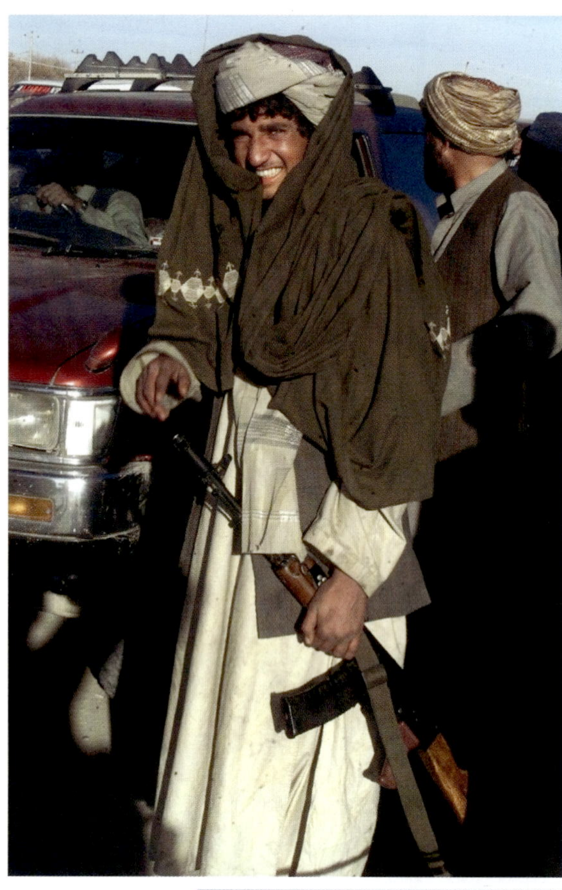

In a matter of hours, Lt Col Tootal and his paratroopers were ordered to the area, even though they were in the middle of preparing to move the bulk of their forces to FOB Robinson and Gereshk to begin securing the 'triangle'. That job was postponed, and they were diverted to head off the Taliban offensive in northern Helmand. The British deployed platoons of paratroopers to protect the district centres and they soon became known as 'Platoon Houses'.

Operation Mutayk

Offensive operations would also take the fight to the Taliban. The first of these was Operation Mutayk, which kicked off on June 4. This saw Tootal leading A Company on a heli-borne raid after what US intelligence had described as a 'high value Taliban target' living in a compound outside Now Zad. The bulk of the RAF Chinook force was mustered for the raid and Apache escort helicopters were on hand, as well as A-10A Warthog ground attack jets belonging to the US Air Force.

What began as a straightforward insertion to set up a 'cordon and search' operation soon turned into a six hour-long firefight. Dozens of heavily armed Taliban were waiting for the Chinooks. As the first paratroopers were emerging from their helicopters

ABOVE: By the summer of 2006 thousands of fanatical Taliban fighters were mounting daily attacks on British bases across Helmand province. (US DOD)

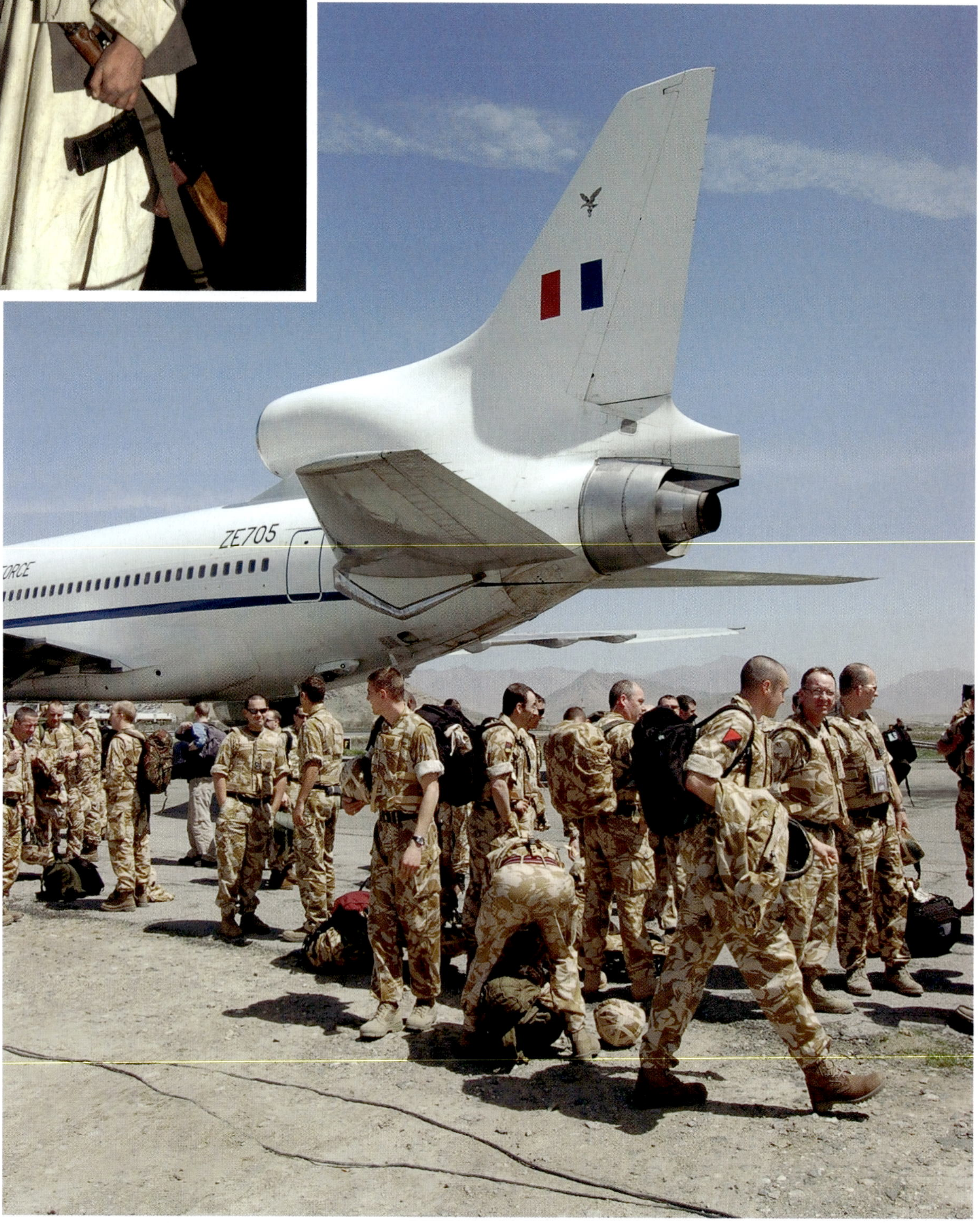

RIGHT: RAF Tristar aircraft carried 16 Air Assault Brigade to Afghanistan in April and May 2006. (TIM RIPLEY)

heavy fire raked the landing zones. They had to fight their way into the compound. Apache gunships were called into strafe Taliban machine gun nests and then the A-10As were ordered in to deal with stubborn resistance. Eventually the Paras managed to sweep through the compound but the 'high value target' had long gone. Every man in the company had engaged the enemy during the bitter battle that left up to three dozen Taliban dead. The heavy resistance and the skill of their opponents had been a bit of shock to the men of 3 PARA, but they had overcome the enemy and had not suffered any casualties. When the Chinooks returned to lift the company back to Camp Bastion morale was sky high. However, over the coming months a series of incidents would start to seriously divert 3 PARA further away from its main mission to secure the 'Triangle' and begin reconstruction tasks.

On June 11, a patrol from 7th Royal Horse Artillery (7 RHA) was ambushed in Sangin and a British officer killed, prompting a rescue mission by 3 PARA's A and B Companies. Two days later A Company was flown north to Musa Qalah to extract a US Army supply convoy that had been ambushed. And when the Taliban killed a political ally of Daoud and several of his bodyguards near Sangin, on June 21, A Company moved into the town to secure the district centre.

Tootal had also managed to get C Company of 3 PARA into Gereshk in a bid to kick start aid operations and it began patrols around the region trying to set up shura with tribal elders to build relationships and win friends.

However, on the evening of June 27, the war in Helmand would ignite and all of the British bases in the region would come under sustained attack. Outside Sangin, a British Special Boat Service (SBS) team raided a 'suspected Taliban compound' on the orders of

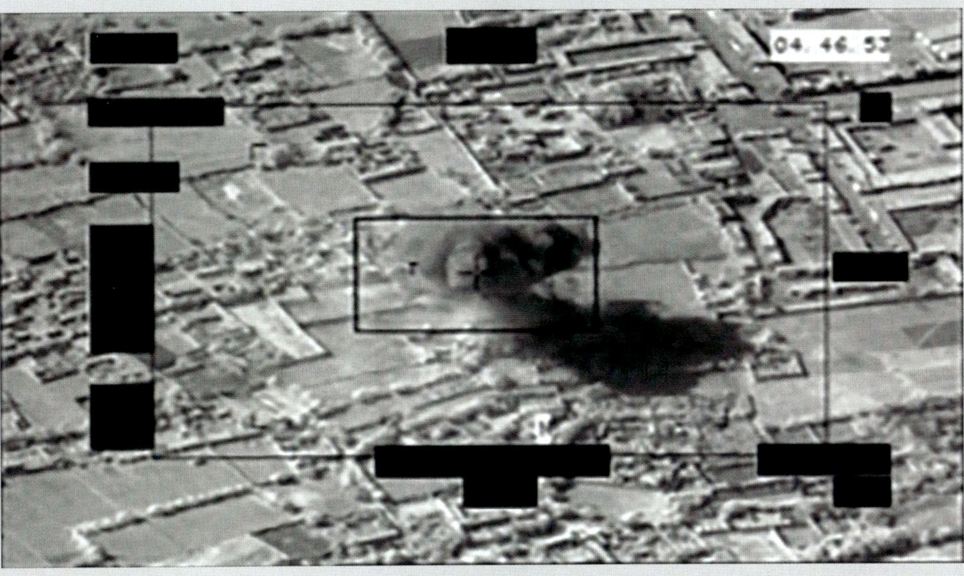

the US special forces command. The assault went badly wrong and two SBS men were killed in a firefight with a large group of Taliban.

A few miles away in Sangin, the paratroopers of A Company had no idea this operation was about to happen. A patrol of British Gurkha troops from FOB Robinson outside the town were sent to help the SBS force move to safety but not before one of their Snatch armoured Land Rovers was hit by a rocket propelled grenade (RPG). The pin-downed troops called up artillery fire from 7 RHA's I Battery to help them return safely to base. They could not find the two dead special forces operatives so at first light B Company was flown out by Chinook from Camp Bastion, under the control of Tootal's tactical headquarters, to put in a large cordon and search operation to try to find the missing men. They were soon discovered along with four dead Taliban fighters.

Further south, on the same day another British patrol was ambushed outside Gereshk as it tried to establish contact with local elders. The platoon from 3 PARA's C Company was lured into the village of Zumbelay by Taliban supporters and then had to fight its way out after the ambush was sprung.

Over the following week British bases in Musa Qalah, Sangin and Now Zad came under sustained attack by large groups of heavily armed, skilled and determined Taliban fighters, backed by hundreds of supplementary fighters recruited from the local population. Fighting intensified as the British troops holding district centres came under hourly sniper, machine gun, mortar, and rocket fire. Casualties mounted as the troops holding these exposed positions found themselves pinned down and unable to move outside their bases except in large patrols. They traded fire around the clock with Taliban fighters and often the only way to diminish the enemy fire was to call up RAF jets to bomb the suspected firing points.

Operation Augustus

At the request of the Americans 3 PARA undertook one last major strike mission in the middle of July, ❯

ABOVE: RAF Harrier GR7 strike jets used laser guided bombs to hit groups of Taliban fighters massing to attack British bases. (MOD/CROWN COPYRIGHT)

BELOW: Its around the clock operations meant that the RAF Harrier detachment at Kandahar airbase in August 2006 was on the verge of running out of bombs. (TIM RIPLEY)

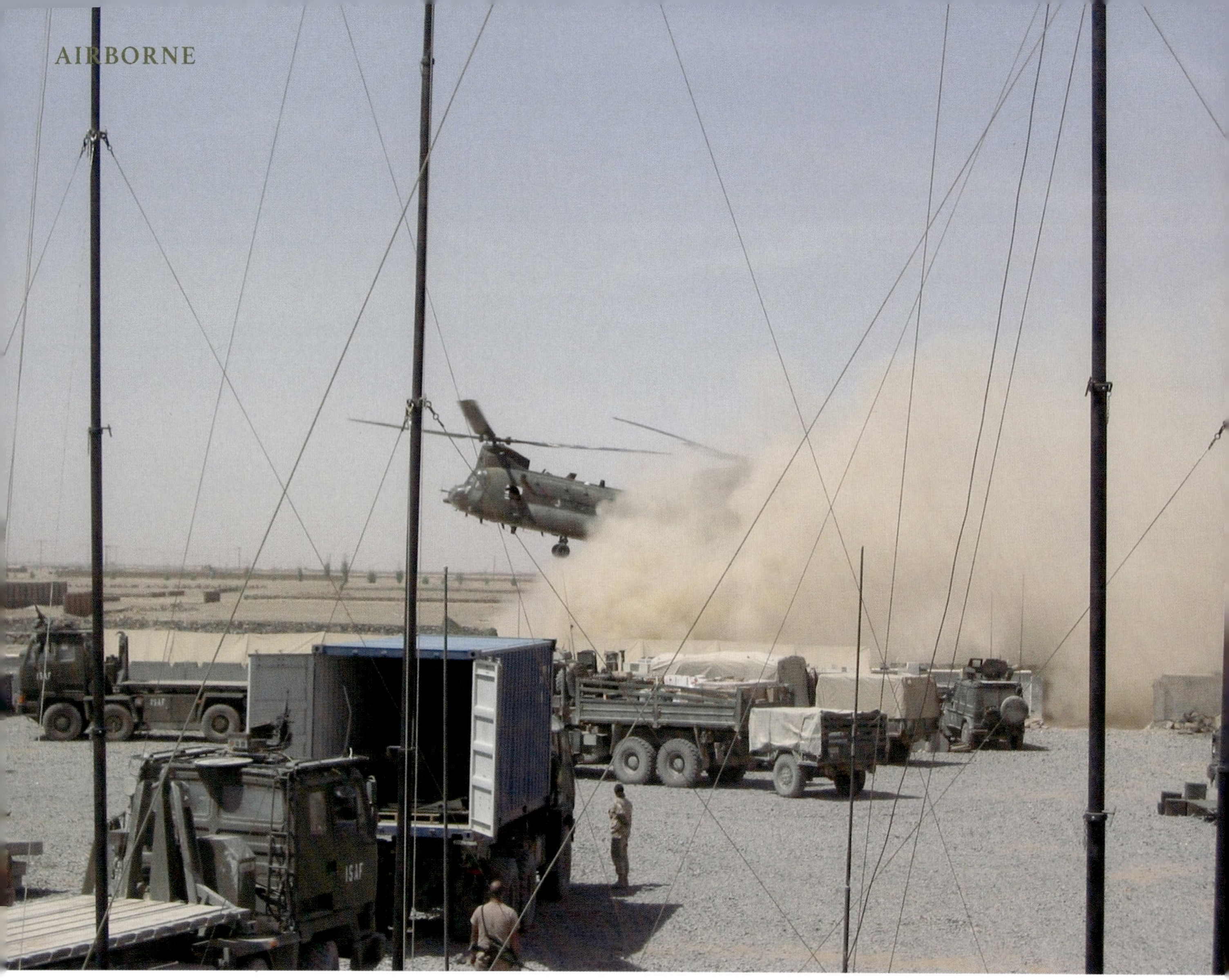

ABOVE: The extreme climate of Afghanistan meant that RAF Chinook crews had to operate to the edge of their helicopter's performance envelope. (CANADIAN DEPT OF NATIONAL DEFENCE)

to hunt down another 'high value Taliban target' near Sangin. Operation Augustus was the biggest 3 PARA operation to date and involved lavish air support, including AC-130 Spectre gunships and General Atomics MQ-1 Predator unmanned aerial vehicles (UAVs), as well as the usual Apache helicopters and RAF Harrier GR7s. A Canadian company mounted in Light Armoured Vehicles (LAV) joined the assault. Taliban fighters put up fierce resistance and the paratroopers came under fire again as they tried to disembark the Chinooks.

"When we go into a hot landing zone the paratroopers had 20 seconds to get off aircraft and they are conditioned to do this" recounted a RAF Chinook pilot who flew during the operation. "We were going into a landing zone when a Para was waiting to get off the aircraft, he was shot but just kept moving to try to get down the rear ramp. The crew had to restrain him, telling him 'you're not going anywhere'."

Again, the 'high value target' was nowhere to be found but a large cache of arms were discovered and destroyed in the compounds secured by 3 PARA and the Canadians.

With British and NATO road convoys now liable to be ambushed or hit with improvised explosive devices (IED), the safest way to resupply the troops in the district centres and bring out wounded was by helicopter. This was not as easy as it seemed. The district centres were in the centre of urban areas, and they did not have room inside them for helicopter landing sites. So, it was impossible to land the big Chinooks safely inside them. The British troops had to mount patrols out of the district centres on to open ground to secure landing sites for any in-bound helicopters. This meant every helicopter mission into the district centres was high risk for the grounds troops and helicopter crews alike. Often, only the presence of Apache gunships circling above the landing sites allowed the Chinooks to get in and out safely.

Changing Role

For senior British commanders it meant the nature of their operation in Helmand had fundamentally changed. Any idea of trying

RIGHT: Army Air Corps Apache AH1 attack helicopters saw action for the first time in Helmand province in May 2006. (AGUSTAWESTLAND)

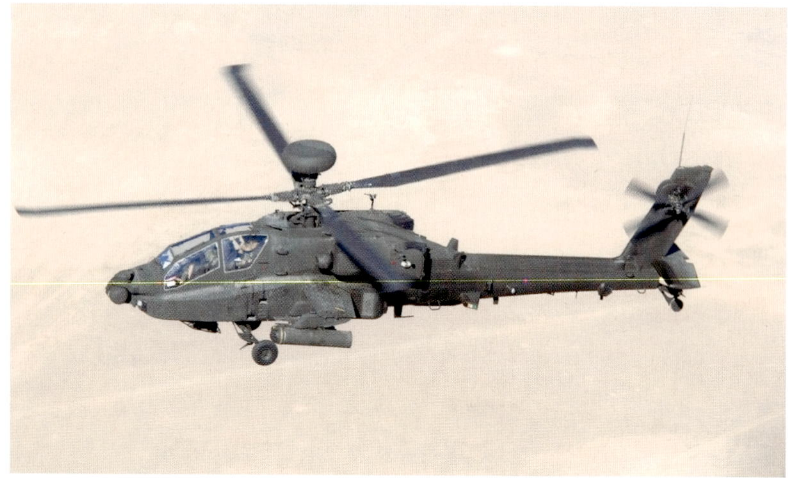

to conduct reconstruction or humanitarian operations was gone.

The bulk of 16 Brigade's combat troops were committed in the district centre and were fighting for their lives. With the summer heat pushing above 50 degrees, food, and water scarce and the troops fighting around the clock, senior officers wondered how long their men could keep fighting.

Brigadier Butler said 3 PARA could not have held out without the efforts of the RAF Chinook crews. "They carried the most risk of anyone here – they can have 40 to 50 guys onboard their helicopters," he said. "I must praise them for keeping going back, it was pretty close at times. They have done some awesome flying". By moving his troops by air, the Brigadier said the Chinooks "saved many lives."

Towards the end of July, the supply situation was getting desperate, so a series of battalion-sized deliberate operations were conducted around the district centres to allow road convoys to get into the beleaguered troops. The bulk of the British Chinook and Apache force were massed for these operations to saturate the local area with more than 400 troops at a time. The first operation around Sangin in mid-July involved two companies of paratroopers, with lavish air support, so the Taliban kept out of the way long enough for a large supply convoy to get into the district centre. Similar events followed in Now Zad and Musa Qalah over the next four weeks. These temporarily relieved the situation but the troops in the district centres were still calling up daily Apache and fixed

The business end of an Apache AH1. Its nose-mounted night-vision system allowed Army Air Corps crews to hunt down Taliban fighters around the clock. (TIM RIPLEY)

wing air strikes to neutralise Taliban rocket and mortar positions.

The combination of determined resistance in the district centres by troops of 3 PARA, as well as small contingents of the Royal Irish Regiment, Royal Regiment of Fusiliers, Gurkhas, Pathfinders, and the Danish Reconnaissance Squadron, along with air support from the Apaches, Chinooks and fast jets was inflicting heavy losses on the Taliban.

Even though the efforts of the Apache and Chinook crews to re-supply the district centres made

many of the headlines during this period, other innovative tactics were being used to defeat the Taliban. The RAF Hercules detachment at Kandahar teamed up with 47 Air Despatch Squadron, to begin air dropping supplies to the beleaguered troops in the district centres.

One senior officer attached to 16 Brigade headquarters in the summer of 2006 recalled: "The Commanding ❯

BELOW: Canadian forward air controllers joined 16 Air Assault Brigade's battles in the summer of 2006, directing air strikes against Taliban fighters. (CANADIAN MINISTRY OF NATIONAL DEFENCE)

16 Air Assault Brigade launched several search and destroy missions to clear Taliban fighters besieging British contingents holding out in Platoon Houses in the north of Helmand province. (MOD/CROWN COPYRIGHT)

RIGHT: The aftermath of an RAF air strike outside of a Platoon House in northern Helmand province. (CANADIAN DEPT OF NATIONAL DEFENCE)

Officer of 3 PARA had far more tasks than he had troops for. Once many of the troops were in forward posts, they were unavailable. So, there was no spare infantry manpower."

This level of combat had not been envisaged by British before 16 Brigade deployed and it was placing a huge drain on the resources of the UK armed forces. The RAF Harrier detachment at Kandahar Airfield almost ran out of bombs at the beginning of September and emergency re-supply flights were ordered to re-stock its bomb dump.

Throughout August the fighting continued at the alarming level of intensity. By late August, British officers were claiming that around 1,000 Taliban had been killed in combat in Helmand, but the enemy seemed to be still fighting with a degree of determination and effectiveness that astounded the British. The other conclusion was that support for the Taliban was growing. By the autumn of 2006, ISAF intelligence officers were estimating that the Taliban could draw on around 12,000 fighters across southern Afghanistan – more than doubling the estimates made earlier in the year.

Butler was by now becoming increasingly concerned at the vulnerability of the casualty evacuation helicopters to Taliban fire and the effect on morale at home in the UK of the loss of a Chinook with major loss of life. The dramatic flight into Musa Qalah district centre by a Lynx to pick up a casualty only highlighted the precarious position of the garrison. In London, the situation was monitored on a daily basis, with growing concern. Senior British officers in Kabul were equally concerned and wanted Butler to pull his men out of the district centres in such a way that did not give a propaganda victory to the Taliban.

In mid September, the tribal elders in Musa Qalah gave the British the excuse they needed to pull out of the town, which had now been heavily damaged during two months of intense fighting. Most of its population had fled to the countryside and the elders approached both the British and the Taliban to ask for a cease fire to allow them to rebuild their town. Both sides had been exhausted by the fighting in northern Helmand and jumped at the chance to pull back when the elders made their offer. Butler flew up to the desert outside Musa Qalah for a shura to broker a deal with the elders. The town was soon quiet, and the deal seemed to stick. Elsewhere around Helmand fighting also

seemed to subside. Both sides were exhausted.

In the middle of October, 16 Brigade handed over duty to Royal Marines of 3 Commando Brigade. Its tour in Afghanistan was hailed as the most intense period of combat faced by the British Army since the Korean War in the 1950s. Between June and September 2006, 19 members of the UK armed forces were killed on the ground and the UK Task Force

suffered a total of 170 casualties during this phase of the fighting.

The level of firepower employed was staggering. Between June and August, 2006, some 260 air strikes had been called in by British troops in Helmand. 3 PARA alone fired 450,000 rounds of small arms and machine gun ammunition, as well as 750 mortar rounds, in some 498 individual engagements. Butler commented that the level of air ❯

ABOVE: Afghan National Army troops were poorly armed and motivated so played little role in 16 Air Assault Brigade's battles in 2006. (NATO)

support used was not what had been originally envisaged. "We did not want to do this, but we needed it for protection," he said.

In the summer 2006 phase of the Afghan campaign the British Army relied on helicopters to an unprecedented degree. Praise for the high level of integration between land forces and helicopters was repeated by Brigadier Ed Butler, who said: "3 PARA would not go anywhere without attack helicopters because of the effect they had on the enemy.

There is an unprecedented bond between 3 PARA and the helicopter crews."

The summer's fighting devastated several of Helmand's major towns and created thousands of refugees. Ambitious plans to kick start reconstruction and humanitarian aid projects just did not happen. In the summer of 2006 Helmand was a battlefield, plain and simple.

Senior officers of 16 Brigade, however, say their fight to hold the

RIGHT: The RAF Chinook detachment in Helmand was the lifeline of 16 Air Assault Brigade's isolated outposts in their desperate battles with the Taliban. (CANADIAN DEPT OF NATIONAL DEFENCE)

district centres formed a 'breakwater', which protected the provincial capital of Lashkar Gar and nearby Gereshk from being overwhelmed by the Taliban 'wave'. Butler described this as "Phase 1 of the campaign," commenting that it was "a five month break in battle – which we won." British troops held their ground and the Taliban failed to seize control of Helmand's main population centres.

Butler attributed this to the fighting spirit of his paratroopers who fought for weeks in desperate conditions, spending 22 hours a day in firing positions in the district centres. "Morale was sky high," he said. "They were still running to the sound of gunfire [even at the end]. The Airborne ethos – jumping out of aircraft – delivered this."

ABOVE: Paratroopers of 16 Air Assault Brigade board a Chinook for the first leg of their journey home in October 2006 after their six month tour of duty in Helmand province. (MOD/CROWN COPYRIGHT)

LEFT: The NATO headquarters at Kandahar airbase controlled the British battle in Helmand province during 2006. This artwork was outside the NATO commander's office, and it summed up the worry that alliance forces had little time to make a difference in Afghanistan. (TIM RIPLEY)

Seize Kyiv

The Battle for Hostomel Airport, Ukraine 2022

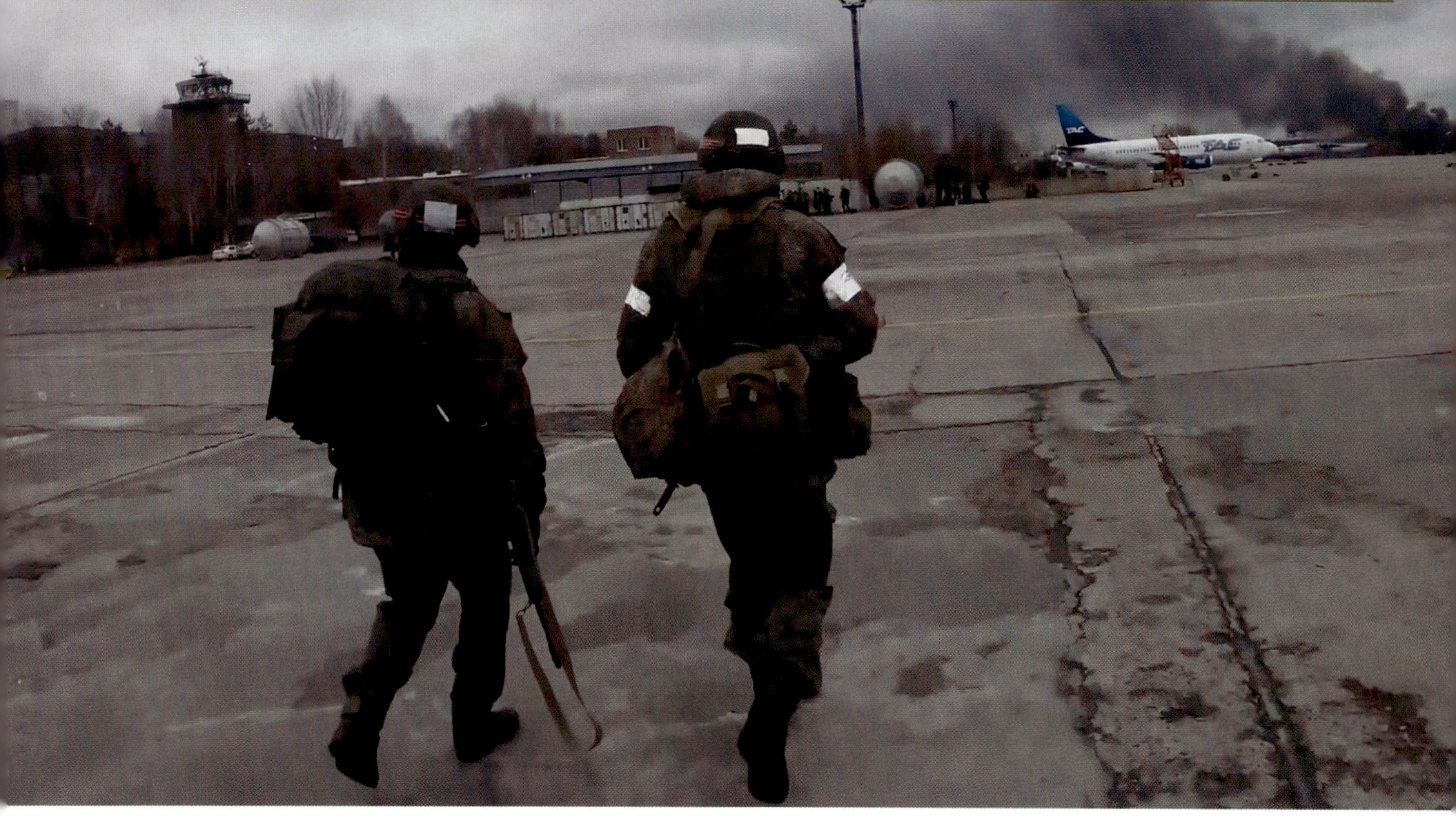

ABOVE: Russian paratroopers landed unopposed at Hostomel airport outside Kyiv in the opening hours of the Kremlin's so-called Special Military Operation in Ukraine. (RUSSIAN MINISTRY OF DEFENCE)

The formation of ten Mil Mi-8 helicopters touched down almost simultaneously in the middle of the main runway of Antonov International Airport in the Kyiv suburb of Hostomel. Within minutes hundreds of Russian paratroopers were in position on the ground protecting the helicopters as they lifted off.

A senior officer then rose and signalled to the paratroopers to move towards the terminal building and surrounding hangers. Within minutes the Russians were clearing the buildings. Anti-tank missile teams were setting up their weapons, ready to repel the inevitable Ukrainian counter attack. A couple of parked airliners were on fire further down the airfield. Overhead, Kamov Ka-52 attack helicopters were circling and occasionally engaging Ukrainian BTR wheeled personnel carriers outside the airport perimeter fence.

The coup d'main operation by the Russian airborne forces, or VDV, to capture an airfield on the outskirts of the Ukrainian capital had begun in a dramatic fashion. Within minutes a US television crew arrived and started to film the Russian troops fanning out to secure the airfield. So far so good for the largest and most ambitious air assault in Russian or Soviet military history. However, within hours fierce Ukrainian resistance would de-rail the operation to seize their capital.

The first sign that the mission was underway was earlier in the morning, when a long line of helicopters could be seen flying down the Dnieper river towards Kyiv. As they neared the city the escorting Ka-52s and Mil Mi-35s gunships and Mi-8 assault helicopters turned west. On the shore, Ukrainian soldiers readied a salvo of Igla heat seeking man portable surface-to-air missiles and started to take aim at the Russian helicopters. One of the Ka-52s was hit and crashed into the river. A Mi-35 also went down. The formation kept going and within minutes, the Mi-8s were landing Russian paratroopers on the runway of Hostomel airport.

RIGHT: For over a month fighting raged around Hostomel airport. Many of the airliners parked at the civilian facility were destroyed in the battle, including the world's largest operational aircraft - the Antonov An-225 Mirya. (OLEKSANDR RATUSHNIAK)

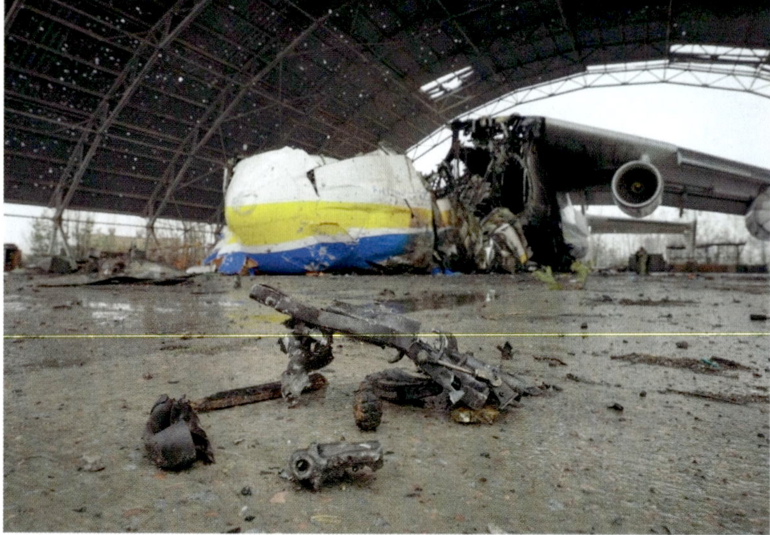

LEFT: More than a 100 Russian combat helicopters were massed in Belarus to support the VDV assault to capture Kyiv. (MAXAR TECHNOLOGIES)

This was all recorded on camera phones of local people and was soon being posted online – they looked like scenes from the epic Vietnam movie, *Apocalypse Now.*

Off Guard

The speed of the daring Russian raid caught the Ukrainian army by surprise and there were no Ukrainian troops defending the airport buildings. This calm would not last long and by the end of the day the Russians troops were fighting off determined Ukrainian counter attacks and diving for cover as artillery fire burst around them.

Once the helicopters had dropped off their paratroopers, they lifted off and headed back to bases in Belarus, over 100km to the north. Ground support crews were waiting at two forward operating bases in fields near the town of Mazyr to refuel and re-arm the in-bound helicopters.

The VDV deployment to Belarus began in January 2022 under the cover of Exercise Allied Resolve 2022, which saw the deployment of an all-arms combat group from the Eastern Military District to the country. A joint Russian-Belarus rapid reaction force was being tested during the exercise, according to Moscow's cover story. Hidden from view of the local media, a large group of VDV paratroopers, predominately from the elite 76th Guards Air Assault Division, arrived at a disused Belarusian airbase, outside the city of Gomel, which was just over the border from Ukraine. The commander of the VDV, Colonel General Andrey Serdyukov arrived in Gomel to lead the operation. He had led the successful Russian intervention in Kazakhstan a few weeks earlier and was considered to be Russian President Vladimir Putin's favourite general. Hundreds of BMD air portable armoured personnel carriers could be seen in satellite imagery of the airbase, being prepared for action. Tents for up to 2,000 troops, or a regiment's worth of paratroopers, were set up at the base. Elsewhere in Belarus two more VDV regiments were training with local troops.

The day before the invasion a large force of Russian Aerospace Force (RuAF) helicopters was photographed in a field operating location in

LEFT: The commander of the VDV, Colonel General Andrey Serdukov, oversaw the initial operation to seize Kyiv but was sacked by Russian President Vladimir Putin after its failure. (RUSSIAN MINISTRY OF DEFENCE)

southeastern Belarus. Satellite images subsequently identified more than 30 assorted helicopters, including Ka-52s and Mi-18s at a temporary base on a road south of Chojniki. The site had also been photographed by local people, who posted images of it

BELOW: After landing by helicopter on the main runway of Hostomel airport the Russian assault force spread out to secure its perimeter to wait the arrival of reinforcements. (RUSSIAN MINISTRY OF DEFENCE)

ABOVE: Russian Aerospace Force Kamov Ka-52 attack helicopters flew escort missions to protect the first wave of troop transport helicopters to reach Hostomel airport. (RUSSIAN MINISTRY OF DEFENCE)

online. Another forward operating location for Russian helicopters was identified in social media images in another field near the town of Mayzr. These sites brought the assault helicopters to within an hour's flying time of Kyiv.

Build Up

Other satellite imagery from this period showed that a large logistic operation was underway to convert a former airfield at Bolshoi Bokov, near Mayzr, into a major helicopter base. This site was not up and running when the war started so several days later the helicopters re-located from the temporary bases to Bolshoi Bokov. A detachment of 15 Mil Mi-26 heavy lift helicopters also took up residence. More than 70 Mi-8s were also moved to Machulishchy airfield, near the Belarus capital Minsk, to be ready to support the Kyiv operation.

During the evening of February 23, convoys of trucks delivered the assault force to roadside helicopter sites near Mayzr in preparation for the mission to Hostomel. Deep in Russia, another VDV battalion was loaded on to 20 Ilyushin Il-76 transports ready to parachute into Ukraine or air land at a captured airfield. More than 8,000 VDV personnel and supporting helicopter crews were now poised to strike against Kyiv.

The Russian plan envisaged the VDV assault force capturing Hostomel airfield and then it would push into the centre of Kyiv to seize the main government buildings. More than 30,000 Russian troops of the Eastern Military District had also been deployed to Belarus and they would race south to Hostomel to link up with the VDV to complete the takeover of the Ukrainian capital. The aim was to topple the Ukrainian government and neutralise its military high command, just as Russian columns were advancing from the north east and south. This was blitzkrieg for the 21st century.

The first wave of helicopters carrying the 45th Guards Spetsnaz Regiment landed relatively safely at Hostomel airport on the morning of

RIGHT: Troops of the VDV's elite 45th Spetsnaz Brigade were landed in the first wave of Russian helicopters to reach Hostomel airport. (RUSSIAN MINISTRY OF DEFENCE)

February 24. A couple of Ka-52s and Mi-35 gunships were shot down but the bulk of the trooping carrying Mi-8s got safely to their objectives.

However, once the Ukrainian military command realised what was happening they started to mobilise troops to try to contain the Russian incursion at Hostomel. Territorial defence units were ordered to head to Hostomel and the nearby suburb of Bucha to try to set up a blocking position. Artillery batteries started to bombard the airfield, forcing the Russian airborne troops to take cover. Buildings and aircraft parked at the airport were set on fire. It was impossible to move around in the open and a follow-up air landing operation to fly in more reinforcements had to be cancelled. Ukrainian National Guard troops massed to attack the airfield, but they were unable to dislodge the VDV units defending the key location.

Fight Back

To the south of Hostomel Ukrainian engineers had set to work to blow up a series of bridges on the main

ABOVE: On February 27, 2022 an attack through Bucha by a VDV column was devastated by a Ukrainian rocket barrage. (UKRAINIAN ARMED FORCES)

BELOW: Ukrainian partisan squads repeatedly ambushed VDV columns trying to move down from Belarus to link up with the paratroopers at Hostomel airport. (UKRAINIAN ARMED FORCES)

RIGHT: Russian tank units of the Eastern Military District pushed south from Belarus to provide the heavy armoured support for the operation to seize Kyiv. (RUSSIAN MINISTRY OF DEFENCE)

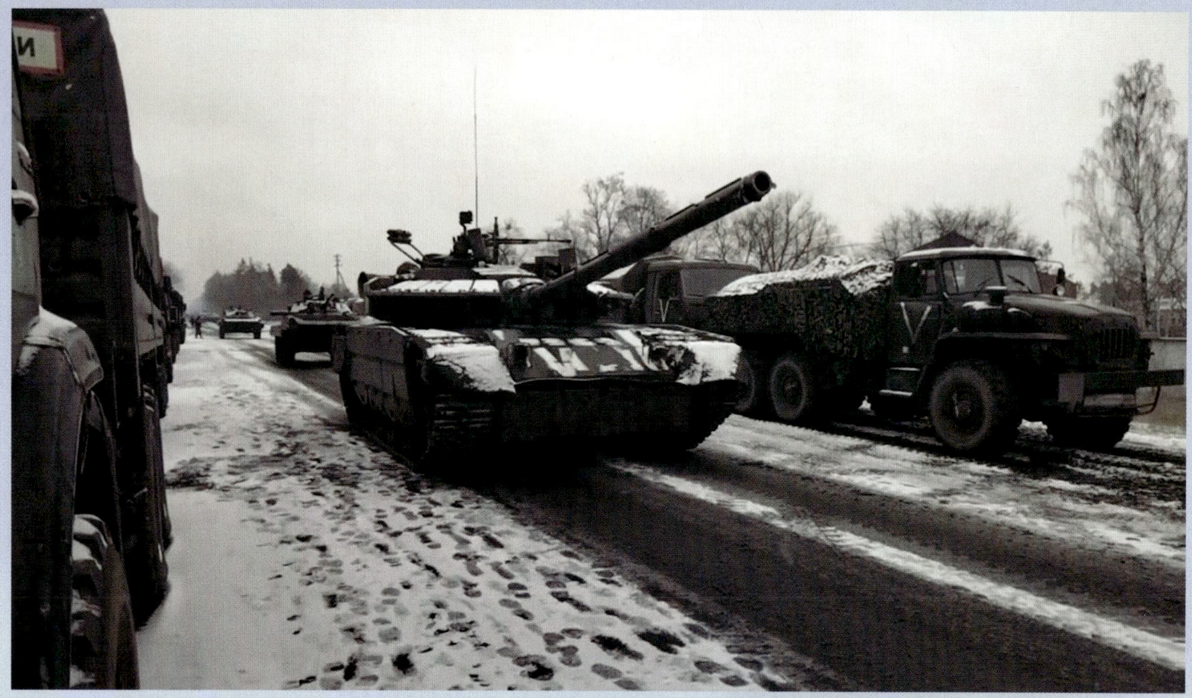

roads into downtown Kyiv. The spans were dropped into the River Irpin, preventing any Russian vehicles driving into the city centre.

Between Hostomel and the Belarus border, more Ukrainian Territorial Defence units tried to interrupt the southwards advance of the Russian relief force. Using ambush and raiding tactics, the Ukrainians knocked out tanks and truck columns, causing traffic jams and tail backs as the Russians stopped to engage the attackers and clear away destroyed vehicles.

Leading the advance from Belarus were columns of VDV

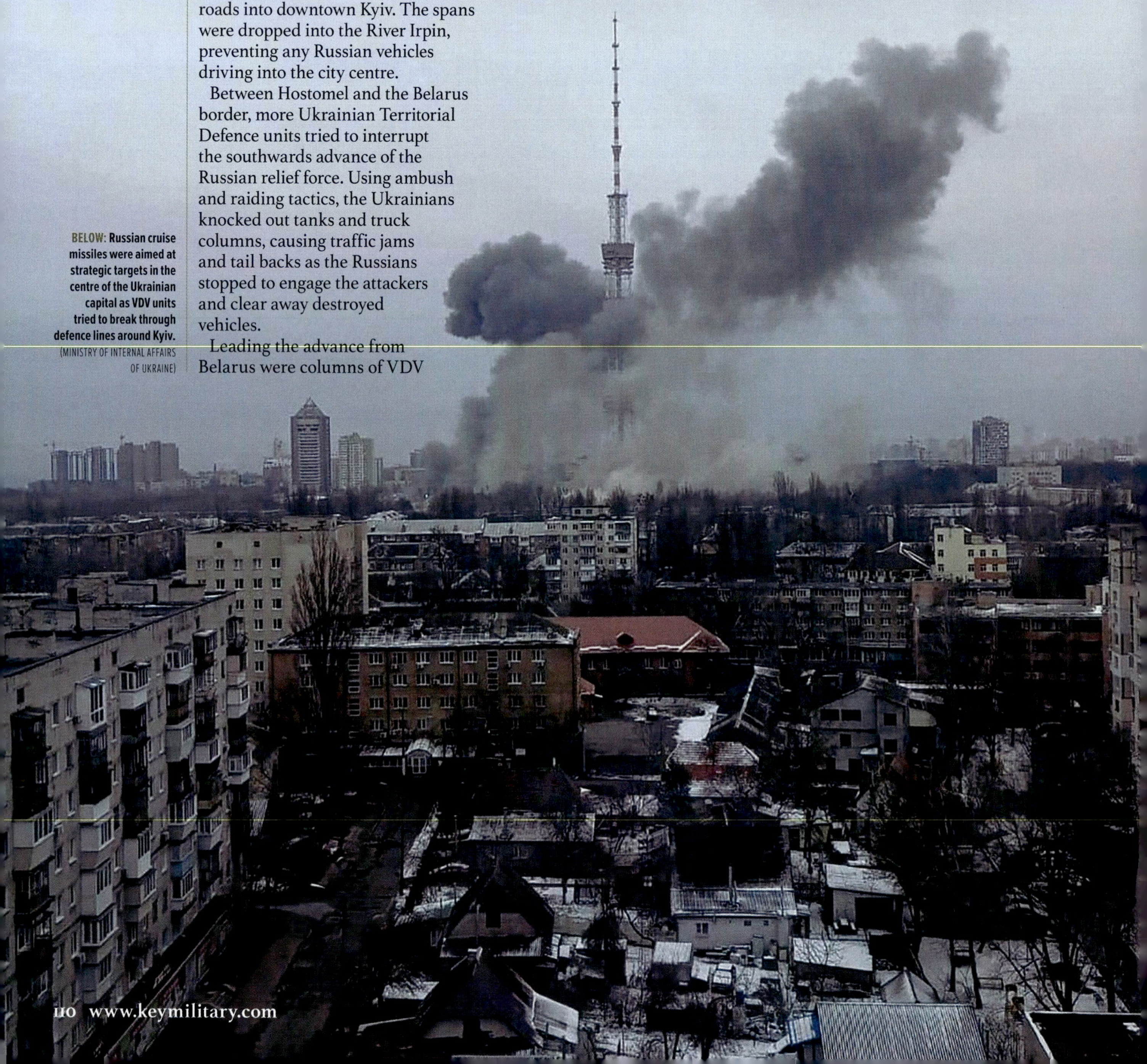

BELOW: Russian cruise missiles were aimed at strategic targets in the centre of the Ukrainian capital as VDV units tried to break through defence lines around Kyiv. (MINISTRY OF INTERNAL AFFAIRS OF UKRAINE)

armoured vehicles and trucks of para-military Russian National Guard units. They managed to weave their way past the Ukrainian resistance to arrive at Hostomel late on the evening of February 24. More reinforcements arrived the following day to continue the build up of Russian forces outside Kyiv.

A determined drive to get into central Kyiv got underway on February 25, but immediately ran into heavy resistance from Ukrainian troops, who fired anti-tank rockets at the Russian columns. This bogged down the Russian advance into a series of small skirmishes in and around the high rise apartment blocks in Bucha.

Russian attack helicopters and Sukhoi Su-25 ground attack jets flew from Belarus to support the VDV offensive and intercept Ukrainian reinforcements moving to join the battle. A video was posted online on February 25 showing a Russian Mi-24 making a daytime low level attack on a convoy of Ukrainian Buk air defence missile systems on a motorway on the eastern outskirts of Kyiv, which left one launcher and several support vehicles burning.

VDV Repulsed

On the morning of February 27, a major VDV operation was launched to assault Bucha by pushing a battalion of BMD armoured vehicles down Vokzalna Street. The VDV commanders appeared confident that the appearance of massed armoured vehicles would send the Ukrainians running for their lives. It was not to be. Ukrainian artillery spotters could not fail to detect such a large force moving in broad daylight. They called up a battery of BM-21 multi-launch rocket launchers to open fire on the VDV column. In matter of minutes dozens of 122mm rockets were landing around the lightly armoured Russian vehicles. The street was turned into

an inferno as, one after another, vehicles exploded. Dozens of Russian vehicles were caught in the kill zone. Hundreds of paratroopers were killed or injured in one of the bloodiest incidents for Russian forces in the Ukraine war. The road to Kyiv was now effectively blocked.

General Serdyukov now set about bringing up more troops, tanks, artillery, and supplies to try to break the Ukrainian defence line along the Irpin river. However, Ukrainian raids and drone strikes on the road down from Belarus hindered his build up. At the same time, the Ukrainians were reinforcing their defences in Kyiv with more anti-tank and anti-aircraft missiles delivered from the west. Artillery fire continued to rain down on Hostomel airfield, preventing fixed wing transport aircraft bringing in supplies and troops. The only way in by air was on Mi-8 helicopters that

dodged through the artillery fire to bring in small groups of personnel and evacuate the wounded.

Russian engineers were brought up to build a PMP pontoon bridge over the Irpin to try to bypass the main Ukrainian defensive position, but it was swiftly destroyed by artillery fire. It was now just not possible for VDV commanders to mass enough troops to achieve a breakthrough without attracting devastating Ukrainian artillery or rocket fire.

Russian casualties started to mount dramatically from snipers, artillery fire and drone attacks. To try to reduce losses to Ukrainian artillery strikes and drone attacks the VDV units started to disperse their BMDs, supply trucks and artillery into garages, industrial sites, and underground car parks.

The fight for Bucha turned into a vicious street battle with Russian and Ukrainian troops trading fire across streets or even ❯

ABOVE: Russian airborne units were all equipped with air droppable BMD-family light armoured vehicles and these saw extensive action around Hostomel airport. (UKRAINIAN MINISTRY OF DEFENCE)

BELOW: Mil Mi-28 attack helicopters provided close air support for VDV units on all fronts in the Ukraine war. (RUSSIAN MINISTRY OF DEFENCE)

ABOVE: Ukrainian National Guard units were rushed to Hostomel to establish a defence line that blocked the Russian advance into downtown Kyiv. (KREACHER)

BELOW: Russian units set up defensive positions to cover their retreat to Belarus after the Kremlin ordered the offensive to capture Kyiv to be called off. (RUSSIAN MINISTRY OF DEFENCE)

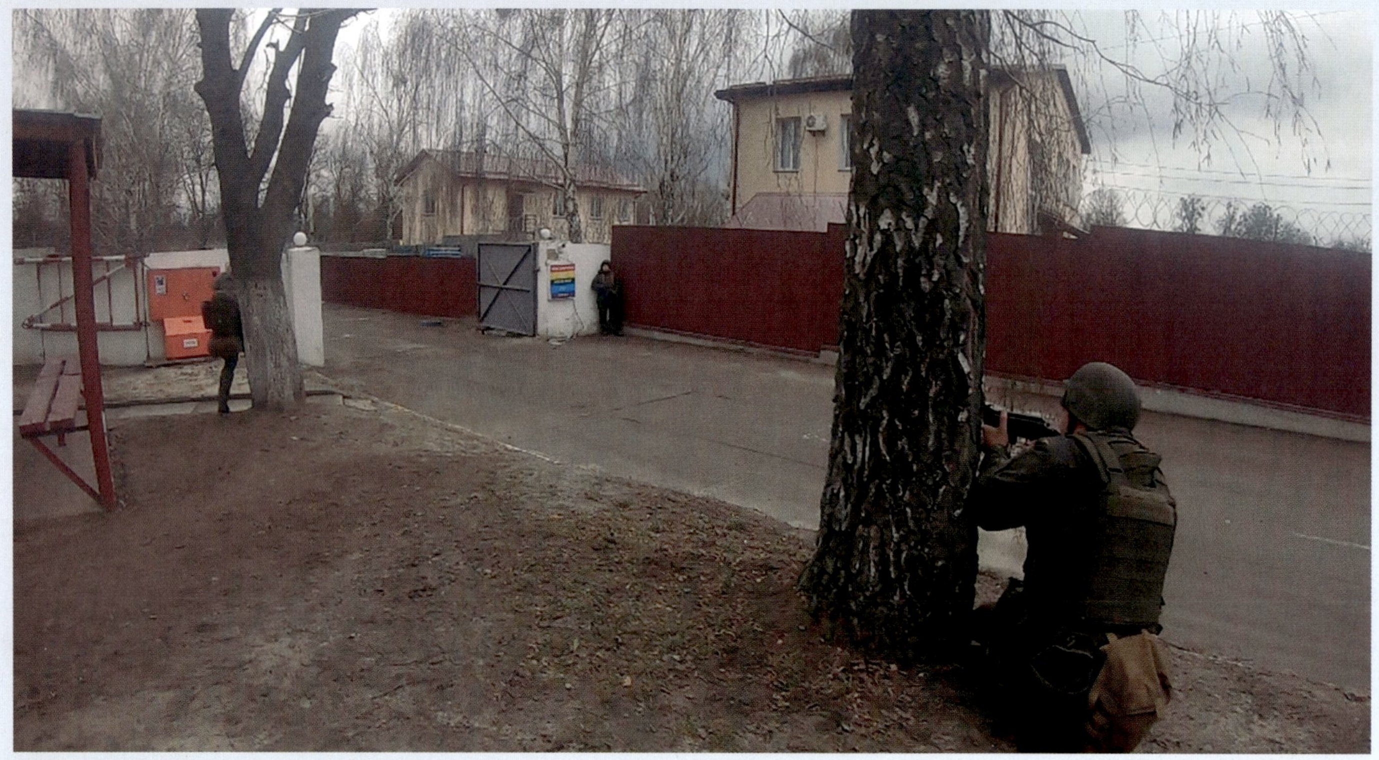

inside buildings. During March, the front lines in the town barely moved but the damage to buildings escalated as both sides traded artillery and rocket fire. Russian occupation forces were accused by the Ukrainians of mistreating and killing civilians during their time in charge of the town.

More units of the Russian 35th Combined Arms Army had now managed to filter down to Bucha and this allowed the majority of the VDV units to pull back to reserve positions to the north of Hostomel. The 98th Guard Airborne Division remained in control of Hostomel airport, but it was still being pounded by relentless Ukrainian artillery fire. Dozens of destroyed VDV vehicles now littered the airport. It had just not been possible to turn it into a functioning airhead to bring in significant reinforcements by air.

D-30 122mm howitzer batteries of the VDV traded fire with their Ukrainian opponents in a bid to reduce the fire landing on frontline Russian positions. And the VDV now had their Orlan-10 mini-drones operating over Kyiv looking for Ukrainian artillery batteries. To try to protect their guns from counter-battery fire, both sides hid them inside forests or industrial buildings and only brought them out to fire when their drones had found a suitable target.

'Scaling Back'

By the third week in March, the Russian high command concluded that their troops outside Kyiv just did not have the combat power to break through the Ukrainian defences around their capital. Days later a Kremlin spokesmen revealed that Russian forces would be 'scaling back their operations around Kyiv' and pulling back to Belarus. The retreat took place in a series of deliberate moves with rear guard units from the 35th Army holding

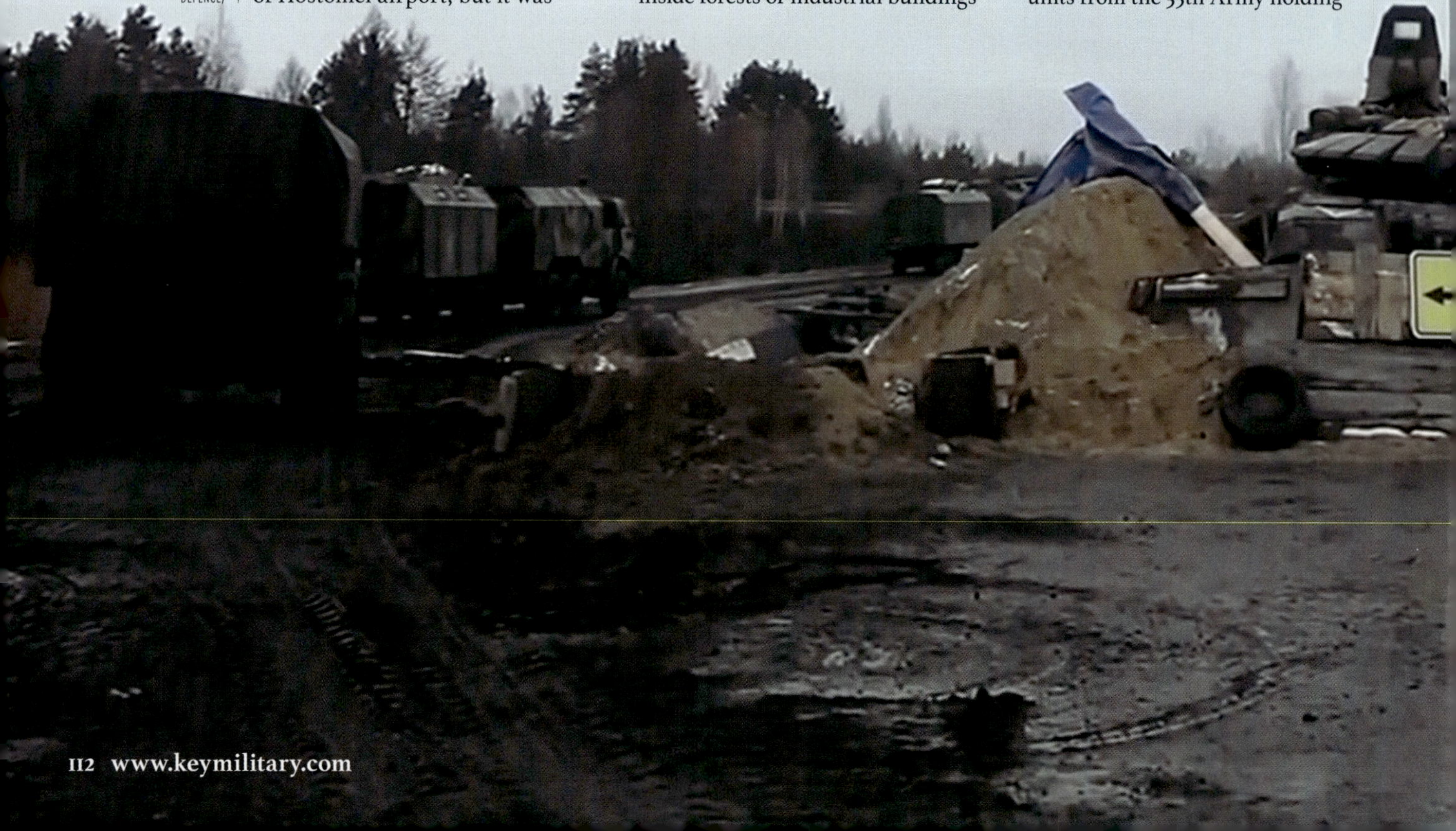

LEFT: Ukraine's President Volodymyr Zelenskyy visited Bucha in the days after the Russian retreat to inspect the devastation. (PRESIDENT OF UKRAINE VOLODYMYR ZELENSKYY OFFICIAL WEBSITE)

spearhead a new Russian offensive in this strategic region.

The Russian airborne assault on Kyiv had failed in its strategic aim of toppling the Ukrainian government in a blitzkrieg strike. While the first wave of VDV units had achieved tactical surprise and captured Hostomel airport, the rapid response of the Ukrainians to block the roads and blow up bridges into Kyiv meant the Russian strike force could not advance much further. Ukrainian resistance along the Russian supply line to Belarus also slowed the build up of the 35th Army's tanks and heavy artillery. The Russian lost the battle to build up combat power outside Kyiv. President Putin was reportedly far from happy at this defeat and news emerged that General Serdyukov had been sacked as commander of the VDV.

the line. Ukrainian troops did not closely pursue and, during the first week of April the final Russian units, including all the main VDV units involved in the Kyiv operations, moved by road into Belarus. Local opposition activists filmed the VDV columns crossing the border flying large airborne forces flags from their BMD vehicles. The paratroopers were sitting on top of their vehicles and waved at the Belarus citizens as they drove towards railheads around Gomel and Mayzr to load their BMDs and other equipment onto troop trains. Some of the vehicles looked battered and damaged but the VDV did not look like a defeated army. It would soon be in action again. VDV units had suffered heavy casualties fighting around Hostomel, but they managed to withdraw from Ukraine in good order and appeared ready to be further operations.

Over the next two weeks, the VDV and Eastern Military District troops were pulled out of Belarus and headed to the Donbas region in southeast Ukraine. They would

BELOW: The area around Hostomel airport was littered with destroyed or abandoned Russian BMD-series vehicles after the VDV withdrew from the battlefield. (UKRAINIAN MINISTRY OF DEFENCE)

By Air to Battle in the 21st century

ABOVE: Parachuting into battle is still a key skill for airborne warriors in the 21st century. (US DOD)

and Paratroopers who jumped into action were lauded for the bravery and daring in these operations, however, their sudden and unexpected arrivals often meant they met negligible resistance so perhaps they were not all a true combat test.

The Russian air assault against Hostomel in February 2022 showed that airborne forces are not all-conquering. When confronted by strong defences - who react rapidly - lightly armed airborne forces still face the challenges their World War Two counterparts faced. So many of the obstacles faced during the German airborne assault on the Hague in 1940 or Crete in 1941 and by the Allied airborne army during the Battle of Arnhem in 1944 seem to have repeated at Hostomel airport.

The vulnerability of British helicopters in Helmand in 2006 and Russian losses in helicopters in Ukraine in 2022, show that modern air defences are a potent threat to air assault forces.

In *Airborne* we have looked back at a range of classic airborne operations and showed that high risk has always been intrinsic to the airborne way of war. The higher the risk, the bigger the pay off.

More than 80 years on from the first mass use of airborne operations in 1940, modern airborne forces continue to have a prominent role in many nation's armed forces.

Airborne operations now encompass not just parachute insertions but also air assault operations by helicopter and air landing in transport aircraft.

Today the capability of the helicopters and aircraft available to move airborne forces into battle are far in advance of those that their forefathers flew in during World War Two or Vietnam. This has expanded the reach of airborne operations and units can be flown thousands of kilometres using aircraft refuelled in mid-air.

US airborne assaults in Grenada, Panama, Afghanistan, and Iraq showed the global reach of strategic parachute operations. The Rangers

RIGHT: Earning the coveted red beret is the culmination of training for the British Army's Parachute Regiment. (MOD/CROWN COPYRIGHT)